EXTERIOR DESIGN IN ARCHITECTURE

Black and white—positive and negative. (Drawing by Aulis Blomstedt)

YOSHINOBU   ASHIHARA

EXTERIOR DESIGN IN ARCHITECTURE

 VAN NOSTRAND REINHOLD COMPANY

NEW YORK CINCINNATI TORONTO LONDON MELBOURNE

Van Nostrand Reinhold Company Regional Offices:
New York   Cincinnati   Chicago   Millbrae   Dallas

Van Nostrand Reinhold Company International Offices:
London   Toronto   Melbourne

Copyright © 1970 by Litton Educational Publishing, Inc.
Library of Congress Catalog Card Number 72-90317

ISBN 0-442-11375-7 cloth
ISBN 0-442-20380-2 paper

Designed by Myron S. Hall III

Published by Van Nostrand Reinhold Company
450 West 33rd Street, New York, N.Y. 10001

16   15   14   13   12   11   10   9   8   7   6   5   4   3   2

CONTENTS

PREFACE

My interest in exterior space was stimulated when I traveled in Europe, especially in Italy, on a Rockefeller travel grant in 1953 and again in 1960. I was surprised to discover that Italians have a sense of space entirely different from that of the Japanese people. Such a discovery, I believe, has contributed a great deal toward developing my fundamental ideas concerning exterior space.

It has been my long-cherished desire, since my first visit to Italy, to write a book on exterior design. In 1960 a Rockefeller Foundation grant enabled me to undertake research into exterior space, mainly in the New York area; at that time I had a chance to visit with Kevin Lynch and Jane Jacobs, who were then undertaking studies similar to mine. I understand that from that research there resulted Mrs. Jacobs' *The Death and Life of Great American Cities.*

Since my full-time work is architectural designing, I have been engaged in the study of exterior space on only a part-time basis; I am afraid, therefore, that my remarks may be sometimes off the point. I think, however, that I have translated my ideas into actuality through my designing activity. I must ask the reader to forgive the fact that the examples of contemporary architecture in this book are from my own works except for a few examples in Chapter 4. I believe that an architect is pre-eminently a man who can express his ideas through his works. All the other examples are from classical architecture or from existing anonymous architecture.

I am indebted to a great many persons for making possible the publication of this study. First and foremost, I would like to thank Dr. Charles B. Fahs, the former director of humanities of the Rockefeller Foundation, for enabling me to undertake research. I would also like to thank my friends, G. E. Kidder Smith and Nathan Glazer, for encouraging me to write this book and for taking great pains to make possible its publication in the United States, and Philip Thiel, a friend who shares an interest in the same subject, for commenting on my manuscript. However, Jean Koefoed of the Van Nostrand Reinhold Company must be chiefly credited with the decision to publish this book in America, and I want to thank him profoundly.

The scheme of this book is based on my *Gaibu Kukan no Kosei* (Exterior Space in Architecture), published in 1962 by the Shokokusha Publishing Company of Tokyo. However, after subsequent research, I have rewritten most of the text. I am grateful to Kunio Komparu, managing director of Shokokusha, for his support of this new book. I am also grateful to Yukio Futagawa for his fine photographs of architecture around the world and to many other photographers; to Hiroshi Ohba, Japan's foremost illustrator, for his beautiful illustrations; to Ikumi Hoshino for taking great pains in translating my Japanese manuscript into English; to Miss Nancy Newman of the Van Nostrand Reinhold Company for co-ordinating many aspects of the editorial work; to Mrs. Saiko Sakamoto, my secretary, for her unfailing assistance; and to Takashi Sawada, a staff member of my firm, and his colleagues for drawing illustrations. Aulis Blomstedt of Finland, one of the friends I respect highly, has drawn a cut for this book; I would like to express my gratitude to him. Last but far from least, I would like to thank my wife, Hatsuko, without whose constant co-operation this book would have been impossible to write.

Yoshinobu Ashihara

THE BASIC CONCEPT OF EXTERIOR SPACE

1 The Formation of Exterior Space

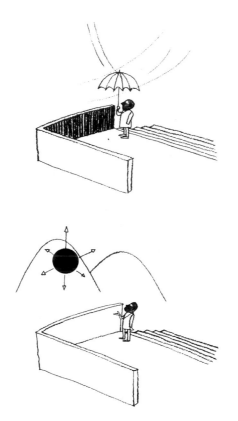

Fig. 1-1. The same space gives different impressions according to the way rain, wind, and sunshine affect it.

Space is basically formed by the relationship between an object and a human being who perceives it. This relationship is primarily determined by sight, but when architectural space is considered, the relationship can be affected by olfaction, audition, and tactility as well. It often happens that the same space gives entirely different impressions according to the way rain, wind, and sunshine affect it.

In our daily life, space is often created in an unintended way. When a family on a picnic spreads out a rug in an open field, for example, there suddenly emerges a place for family enjoyment, a space carved out from nature; when the rug is folded up, there remains nothing but the open field. When a man and a woman, walking in the rain, open an umbrella, there is immediately created under the umbrella a world of "just you and me"; when the umbrella is folded up, the intimate space for the two persons disappears. When a crowd gathers around a speaker in the open air, a space filled with tension develops around the speaker; when the speaker ends his speech and the crowd disperses, such space ceases to exist. Space is thus such

Fig. 1-2. When a family on a picnic spreads out a rug, there emerges a space carved out from nature.

Fig. 1-3. When a couple walking in the rain opens an umbrella, there is created under the umbrella a world of "just you and me."

Fig. 1-4. When a crowd gathers around a speaker, a space filled with tension develops around the speaker.

an interesting phenomenon that it deserves our serious study. The ancient Chinese philosopher, Lao Tzu, said felicitously, "Though clay may be molded into a vase, the essence of the vase is in the emptiness within it."[1] Lao Tzu's words are exceedingly pregnant. Architects, however, must not forget that clay is needed in order to create the empty space in the bowl.

Generally speaking, interior architectural space is delimited by three planes—a floor, a wall, and a ceiling. It must be admitted that recently architecture in which it is difficult to distinguish between the three planes has been built, such as shell structures where walls and ceilings are integrated, and cavelike structures in which floors flow into walls and ceilings. Although we are now over the threshold into the space age, architectural space still must have a floor. In exterior space as well as in interior space, texture, pattern, form, color, size, difference in floor height, etc., are key design elements, which will be enlarged on later.

When architects create architectural space, not with umbrellas or rugs, but with architectural materials, floors, walls, and ceilings are all important elements. Suppose, for example, that we have built a brick wall on ordinary flat ground where sunshine sparkles. In countries in high latitudes, such a brick wall creates on the sunny side a space where a couple of lovers can engage in intimate conversation, leaning against the wall, while on the reverse side there is cold space without any sunshine. When the wall is removed, the ground will return to its natural form. Suppose, further, that something like a canopy is hung over a piece of empty ground. In warm latitudes, a resting place to protect man from the merciless sun will be created under the canopy. When the canopy is cleared, the ordinary ground will be restored. Thus, it is possible to create architectural space on a natural piece of ground by bringing into existence a wall or canopy. And the way in which the wall or canopy is brought into existence determines to a great extent the quality of the space.

What, then, is exterior space in architecture? First of all, it is space created by delimiting nature. Exterior space is separated from nature by a frame, and is not nature itself, which extends infinitely. It is a man-made exterior environment with a purpose; it is a meaningful space as well as a part of nature. Designing exterior space, therefore, refers to the technique of creating such exterior space. Surrounded by its frame, exterior space develops within itself a centripetal order; positive space, brimming with human intentions and functions, is created inside the frame. On the other hand, nature is centrifugal space, extending to infinity, and it is regarded as negative space. The concept of exterior space in the architect's mind may be different

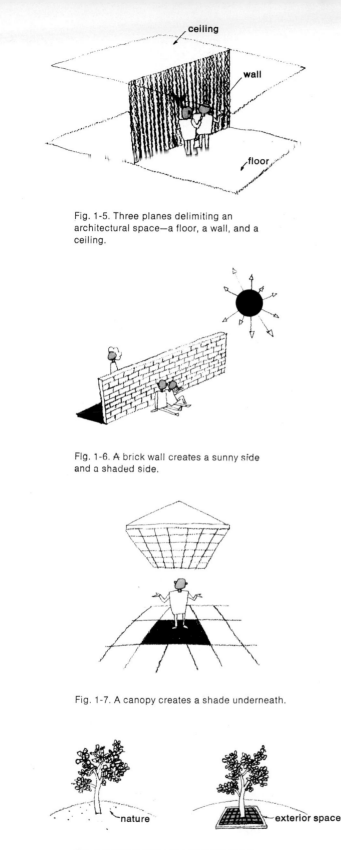

Fig. 1-5. Three planes delimiting an architectural space—a floor, a wall, and a ceiling.

Fig. 1-6. A brick wall creates a sunny side and a shaded side.

Fig. 1-7. A canopy creates a shade underneath.

Fig. 1-8. When a tree is surrounded by a fence, exterior space comes into existence around the tree.

Exterior space is created by delimiting nature,
aerial view of Ise Shrine.
(Photo by Yukio Futagawa)

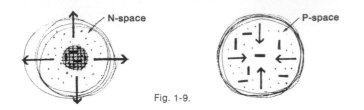

Fig. 1-9.

Centrifugal space extending infinitely.   Centripetal space inside the frame.

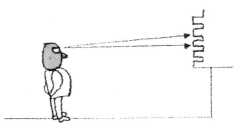

Fig. 1-10. It is necessary to know the relationship between the materials and how they look at a certain distance.

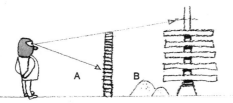

Fig. 1-11A. If a wall is higher than eye level, space is separated into A and B.

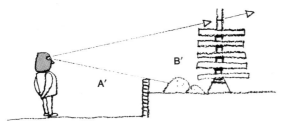

Fig. 1-11B. If a wall is lower than eye level, A' and B' are united into one.

Opposite:
Architecture without a roof, aerial view of the city of Siena.
(Photo by Yukio Futagawa)

from that conceived by the landscape architect, for "exterior space" is to the architect another name for "architecture without a roof." In other words, if the whole building plot is considered as a work of architecture, portions with a roof being considered indoor space and portions without a roof, outdoor space, it is obvious that this outdoor space is architectural space and that it differs in nature from a garden or open space.

As mentioned above, architectural space is delimited by three planes, a floor, a wall, and a ceiling. Exterior space, regarded as "architecture without a roof," however, must be delimited by only two planes—a floor and a wall; in other words, it is space created through the use of only two dimensions, one element fewer than in the creation of interior architectural space. This makes the floor and wall planes all the more important determinants in this type of design.

In order that exterior space may qualify as "architecture without a roof," not as infinitely extensive nature, planning should be carefully undertaken. Since exterior space is designed with only the two dimensions, full attention should be paid to the design of the horizontal plane. Knowledge is also essential concerning the relationship between the materials and how they look at a certain distance, for any wall will be observed from a far greater distance than will an interior wall. Decisions on whether the wall should be higher or lower than eye level are also important; and the ratio of the height of the wall to its distance from the viewer should be studied. In the design of exterior space, more trees, water, and natural stones will be used than in the design of interior space; ceramics, bricks, cut stones, and outdoor sculptures and furniture that withstand exposure to rain, winds, and sun can be used. Close attention should be given to the direction from which sunshine comes, for its use can add nuances to space, and lighting is as important in determining the nocturnal mood as it is in interior designs.

The Piazza del Campo in Siena[2] was developed, centering on the Palazzo Pubblico, over a period of two centuries beginning around the late eleventh century; the nine sectors paved later are inclined toward the Palazzo Pubblico; Jacopo della Quercia's Fonte Gaja, whose water gushes forth from a previously installed pipeline, is appropriately located in the elevated part. The whole plaza is designed to suit any kind of gathering or festivity; even today a large number of citizens come yearly to the plaza to watch the medieval Palio.[3] The buildings surrounding the plaza vary in height and in the layout of their windows, but "unity through diversity" has been achieved. If one looks at the aerial photograph of the plaza, he cannot help feeling

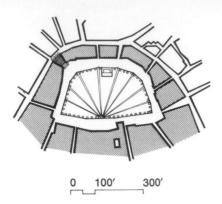

0   100'   300'

Fig. 1-12. Plan of the Piazza del Campo, Siena.

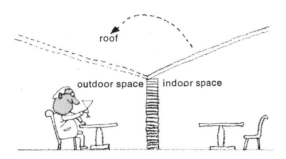

Fig. 1-13. Sipping wine in the corner of an Italian plaza, you experience an illusion that the roofs of buildings come over the plaza, and indoor space and outdoor space are reversed.

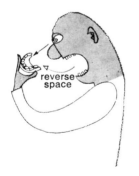

Fig. 1-14. A cast of a person's set of teeth is "the reverse space" of his dentition.

that it is truly "architecture without a roof." The Piazza del Campo still functions as an urban core because of its splendid exterior space. The medieval Italian city is centripetal space surrounded by walls, and the whole city is like one house, with the plaza serving as a kind of living room for the city as a whole. Kidder Smith says in *Italy Builds:*

> The square, or piazza, in Italy is far more than so many square feet of open space; it is a way of life, a concept of living. Indeed, it might be said that the Italians have the smallest bedrooms but the largest living rooms in Europe. For the square, the street and the sidewalk are their living space, their playrooms, their front "parlor" . . . Their tiny, ill-lit, crowded flats are primarily spots for sleep, love, meals and possessions. Most leisure time is spent, indeed must be spent, outside.[4]

Another interesting thing about the Italian plaza is that there is hardly any difference between indoor and outdoor space except for the existence or nonexistence of a roof; almost no trees are planted, and the outdoor floor is paved with beautiful patterns. Thick, solid walls of masonry construction with small windows stand between indoor and outdoor space and do not allow such penetration of space as is observed in Philip Johnson's Glass House. Sitting in the corner of such an Italian plaza and sipping somewhat sleep-inducing wine, one half-closes his eyes; then he experiences an illusion that the roofs of buildings come over the plaza, and that indoor space and outdoor space are reversed, with hitherto interior space turning into exterior space and hitherto exterior space turning into interior space.

Such a reversibility of interior and exterior space is extremely suggestive for the study of space, and it may be as well to conceive of the idea of "reverse space." When one goes to a dentist and has him make a cast of one's teeth, that cast is a kind of "reverse space." Since on a map of an Italian city the white spaces not occupied by buildings are all streets and plazas—in other words, buildings directly abut on streets—it would cause no harm from the point of view of reverse space even if the black and white sections on the map were reversed. It is important, in designing exterior space, that the designer express his intentions to the full even in this "reverse space." Only when the architect gives sufficient attention not only to the space occupied by the buildings he designs, but also to space not occupied by his buildings—that is, when he pays attention to reverse space— only when he designs the surroundings of his buildings as positive space, or only when he conceives of the whole building plot as one piece of architecture and of the parts without a roof as exterior space, does he really begin to design exterior space.

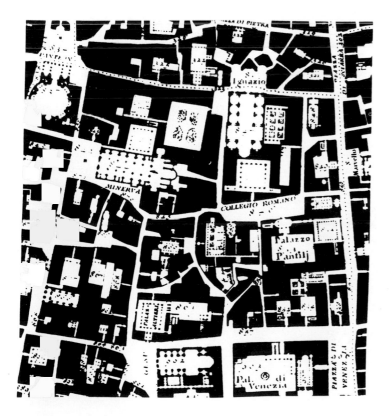

Fig. 1-15A. The maps of Italian cities indicate buildings and spaces not occupied by buildings (streets or plazas) in black and white. From the map of Rome drawn by Giambattista Nolli, 1748.

Fig. 1-15B. The maps of Japanese cities, like the old Edo map shown here, indicate the relationship between building sites and streets, but do not show the location of buildings on the sites. From *Kohan Edo-zu Shusei* (A Collection of Old Edo Maps), Vol. 4 (Tokyo: Chuo Koron Bijutsu Shuppan, 1958), p. 35.

Piazza del Campo viewed from the east.
(Photo by Paolo Riani)

The same place when the Palio is held.
(from *Life*, Vol. 50, No. 26, June 30, 1961)

2 Positive Space and Negative Space

There are two kinds of architectural space, one whose vector focuses inward on the center, and the other whose vector diffuses outward from the center. If we view space B surrounding object A as full space, we can regard B as positive toward A and define B as positive space (P-space) in its relation to A. If we view space B surrounding object A as natural space without human intentions, we can regard B as negative toward A and define B as negative space (N-space) in relation to A.

Fig. 1-16. Positive space and negative space.

When the painter draws a still life in accordance with the techniques of traditional Western oil painting, he applies colors fully to the background as well as to the figure and leaves no space unpainted; his intentions are manifested all over the canvas. We can regard the background in such a painting as P-space. On the other hand, the background in an Oriental black-and-white painting is unpainted, empty, infinite, diffuse space. Such space can be regarded as N-space. Although we thus have the two different concepts of space, N-space may turn into P-space, undergoing a qualitative transformation, and P-space may become N-space, assimilating itself with nature in the course of a long period of time.

The positivity of space indicates the existence of human intentions or of planning with regard to the space. From the viewpoint of space theory, planning means that first boundaries are determined and then order is built inward toward the center. On the other hand, the negativity of space implies that the space is spontaneous and has no plan. In terms of space theory, nonplanning refers to the outward proliferation of disorder. Thus P-space is centripetal, and N-space, centrifugal.

How can the concepts of P-space and N-space be applied to actual works of architecture?

If object A—a distinct object, such as an obelisk or a piece of sculpture—is placed in an environment extending, like nature, to infinity, the space surrounding object A can be regarded as N-space in relation to the object. In this case, however, object A can be considered unique and monumental as well. On the other hand, if object A is an independent object such as a pillar or a freestanding fireplace, the living space surrounding object A is fully functioning and can be regarded as P-space. In this sense, it may be said that indoor space in architecture is P-space with internal functions. If we view objects A_1, A_2, and A_3 in Figure 1-16III' as individual architectural works, they are like a village that has developed spontaneously along a road; the space surrounding them is infinite and diffuse and may be considered N-space. This kind of space can extend itself infinitely if need arises, although the lack of a plan may lead to confusion; on the other hand, such space may result in an expression of humanity often overlooked in planning. In Figure 1-16III and the photograph of the planned residential area in Harlow, England, clusters of buildings are surrounded by full space like the background in an oil painting; the surrounding space, which is pregnant with human intentions and planning, can be regarded as P-space. Since this space has clear-cut boundaries and cannot extend outward, the intensification of functions within the boundaries may be expected and exterior space will be formed.

Fig. 1-17A. From the point of view of space theory, planning can be compared to pouring water into a cup, while the lack of planning can be compared to spilling water on the floor. The former is centripetal, and the latter, centrifugal.

Fig. 1-17B. One couple finds one day that they have three children, while another couple has three children according to plan. The basic difference between the two couples is whether they planned to have three children or not.

Planned residential area in Harlow, England.
Courtesy of Architectural Press Ltd., London.
(Photo by Photoflight Ltd.)

Opposite:
A village that has developed spontaneously
along a road in Yamato, Japan.
(Photo by Yukio Futagawa)

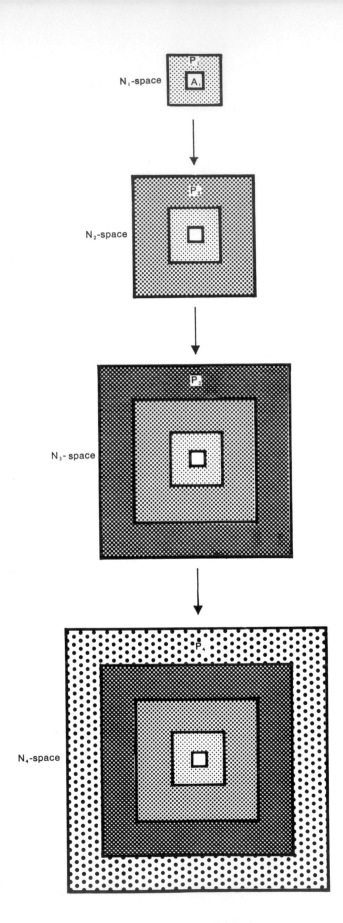

A. When P_1-space exists around A_1, N_1-space emerges around P_1-space.

B. If N_1-space is transformed into positive space, the space surrounding it will become N_2-space.

C. If N_2-space is transformed into positive space, the space surrounding it will become N_3-space.

D. A similar process of transformation is repeated.

Fig. 1-18. A succession of transformations of N-space into P-space.

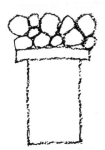

lintel construction

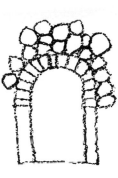

arch construction

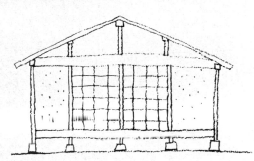

post-and-beam construction

Even when a full positive space around object A_1, N_1-space exists outside the frame of this P_1-space. If the surrounding N_1-space becomes positive, a hitherto negative place like N_1 will become P_2-space. Outside this P_2-space, however, another negative space will still exist. Thus, the emergence of P-space and N-space is repeated endlessly. For architects, the important question is where to delimit the territory of their work in designing exterior space. As this territory is expanded, planning for it will become city planning, regional planning, national land planning, or even universe planning, far beyond the boundaries within which the architect normally works.

Next, let us consider the penetration or permeation of space. In masonry construction such openings as windows and doors are carved out from walls by the use of lintels or arches. On the other hand, in post-and-beam construction, which is used in traditional Japanese wooden architecture, all the area except posts and beams can be openings, and the architect's main concern is not how to carve out openings but how to fill in openings. Generally speaking, in houses of post-and-beam construction, openings are large and interior space interpenetrates exterior space with few clear-cut boundaries between them.

In traditional Japanese wooden architecture, harmony with, rather than opposition to, nature has been striven for. Japanese gardens at first glance look very natural; on closer examination, however, they reveal themselves to be very elaborate, man-made miniatures of nature and to be different from N-space, which is true nature. It may be said that Japanese gardens are PN-space, which has resulted from architecture, or P-space, permeating gardens. Japanese gar-

Fig. 1-19. In masonry construction, openings are carved out from walls with the use of lintels or arches. In post-and-beam construction, all the spaces except the posts and beams can be openings, and the architect's concern is not how to carve out openings but how to fill in openings.

Post-and-beam construction, Katsura Detached Palace, Kyoto, Japan.
(Photo by Yukio Futagawa)

Opposite:
Masonry construction with arched openings, Dubrovnik, Yugoslavia.
(Photo by Yukio Futagawa)

The Rock Garden of Ryoanji Temple, Kyoto, Japan.
(Photo by Yukio Futagawa)

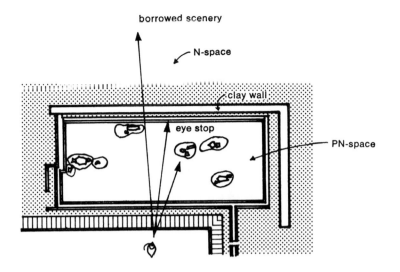

Fig. 1-20. Plan of the Rock Garden of Ryoanji Temple, Kyoto.

dens require frames to separate them from true nature. At Ryoanji Temple in Kyoto, for example, the clay walls with roof tiles acting as a frame are needed so that space can penetrate or permeate from indoors to the rock garden; without these walls the design of this garden would be much less striking. In other words, the garden is PN-space discreetly designed by taking into consideration all the space surrounded by the walls. Outside the walls, of course, there exists N-space, which has no direct relation with Ryoanji Temple. In the technique of Japanese landscaping called *shakkei* (borrowed scenery), however, the views of distant hills and trees are carefully incorporated in the garden design, and the space surrounding the garden is more than mere N-space; if television towers or factories, which belong to a different order, intrude into the borrowed scenery, the quality of PN-space will deteriorate considerably.

It is interesting to note that the architecture of masonry construction, in which hardly any interpenetration of space exists, can stand as a part of the landscape even when standing alone in nature, whereas steel-and-glass houses and Japanese wooden architecture, in which the penetrability of space is high, can hardly ever become a part of the landscape unless frames exist outside buildings.

church

shrine

Fig. 1-21. Ecclesiastical structures often directly abut on streets, but Japanese Shinto shrines are always surrounded by fences.

Ecclesiastical structures whose walls are solid and do not allow the penetration of space are self-contained in that one can perform religious rituals inside the structure; thus, for instance, the cathedral at Chartres can stand in isolation, exposed to nature. A church can stand closely surrounded by the walls of other buildings. In Japanese Shintoist architecture, however, the shrine cannot stand alone; unlike the Christian church, it needs the precincts as a frame. The shrine hall is a place where a Shintoist god is enshrined and into which worshipers are not usually allowed to enter. It is similar to the altar in a Christian church; since one cannot approach it, it has, in spatial terms, the same meaning as a piece of sculpture or an obelisk. It must, therefore, be placed in the midst of a dignified and religious atmosphere; it needs the precincts and should not be directly exposed to nature, as is a building of masonry construction. Some shrines are surrounded by fences and trees; some precincts are reached by steep flights of steps leading far above eye level. Since one cannot see through the space above one's eye level, the expectation of something solemn is awakened in the mind. The *torii* (Shintoist gate) can also give meaning to space through the simplest design and make someone who passes through it feel that he has entered the special area of the shrine precincts. In spacious shrine precincts, he comes to the end of an approach after passing the first *torii*. When he turns at a right angle, the second *torii* comes into view. Only after passing the second *torii* does he enter the inner part of the premises and approach the main shrine hall. After cleansing his mouth and hands, he worships by turning toward the hall.

Generally speaking, Japanese wooden houses do not directly face the street but are surrounded by fences. Since the garden is invisible from the street, it is ruled by the order inside the house. On the other hand, American suburban houses are surrounded by green lawns and flower beds; gardens are integrated into such an exterior order as is represented by streets, and they become objects of appreciation

A church surrounded by N-space.
(Photo by Yoshinobu Ashihara)

Meiji Shrine, Tokyo, Japan.
(Photo by Yukio Futagawa)

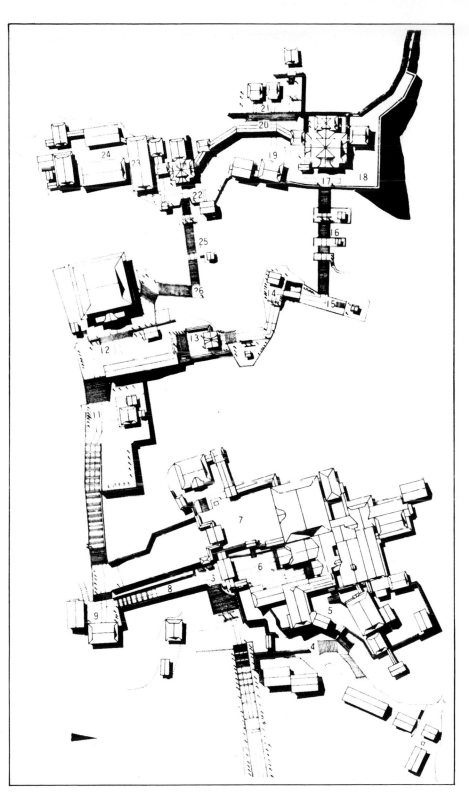

Fig. 1-22. Kompira Shrine is one of the best-known shrines in Japan. To reach the shrine hall, worshipers have to pass through *torii* gates, go up steps, and make sharp turns in a planned sequence of spaces. From *Nihon no Toshi Kukan* (Japanese Urban Space) (Tokyo: Shokoku-sha, 1968), p. 114.

Opposite:
A *torii*—Shintoist gate, Japan.
(Photo by Yukio Futagawa)

Fig. 1-23. Relationship between houses and gardens.

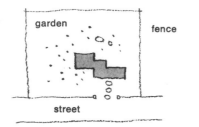

In Japan, gardens are usually part of an interior order.

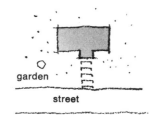

In America, gardens seem to belong to an exterior order.

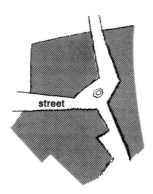

In Italy, houses face streets or plazas, and there are no gardens between them.

to passers-by: Thus the neighborhood as a whole is beautiful. In American suburbs, indeed, the gardens are sometimes not clearly visible from inside the houses. In the case of Japanese houses, gardens are ruled by an interior order, and fences serve as boundaries to separate interior from exterior space; in the case of American suburban houses, gardens are ruled by an exterior order, and the interior-exterior boundaries exist where houses and gardens meet. In the case of Italian houses, on the other hand, there are no gardens at all; thick walls of masonry construction serve as interior-exterior demarcations.

Standing alone, a piece of architecture tends to be sculptural or monumental. When there are two pieces of architecture, however, a force intervening between them begins to work. As pieces of architecture increase in number, forming a group, and as the plan becomes complex in terms of convexity and concavity, exterior space tends to become P-space.

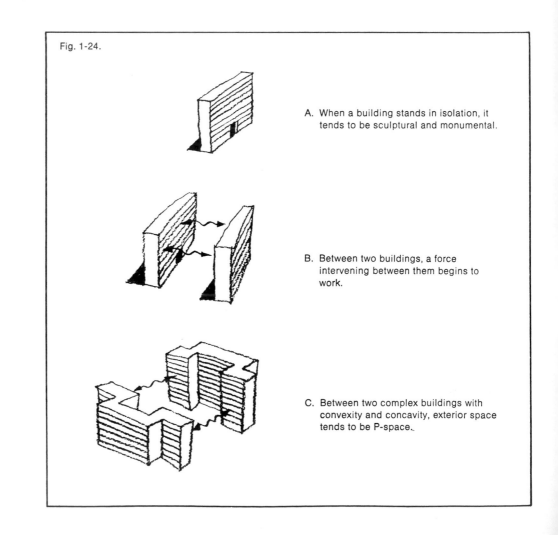

Fig. 1-24.

A. When a building stands in isolation, it tends to be sculptural and monumental.

B. Between two buildings, a force intervening between them begins to work.

C. Between two complex buildings with convexity and concavity, exterior space tends to be P-space.

Fig. 1-25A.

N-space

When object A and the reverse space B balance each other beautifully, monumentality is enhanced.

When other objects which may disturb the reverse B emerge around the same object A, monumentality is reduced.

There seem to be two kinds of monumentality. First, monumentality is achieved when monuments are clearly isolated from other objects; monumentality is formed, for instance, by such vertical elements as are represented by an obelisk or a tower and by N-space surrounding vertical elements. When there is no interpenetration between the forms of monuments and the N-space, which is reverse space, and when the two balance each other beautifully, monumentality becomes unique and its quality is enhanced. When, however, other objects that may disturb the reverse space are present around monuments, the balance between the forms of monuments and the reverse space is upset, and monumentality is drastically reduced. The second kind of monumentality is achieved by a cluster of architectural designs. Suppose, for example, that there are two objects A and B as in Figure 1-25B. An enclosing force works between A and B, bringing into existence PN-space, which is neither P-space nor N-space; thus a complex space combining PN-space (between A and B) and N-space (around A and B) is created.

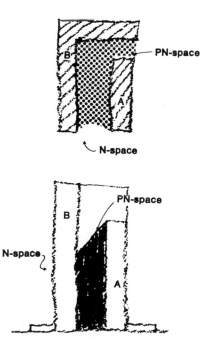

Fig. 1-25B. Complex monumentality: (N + PN) space.

Primordial monumentality.
Obelisk of Place de la Concorde, Paris, France.
(Photo by Yukio Futagawa)

Fig. 1-26. Complex monumentality. Section of the First Prize Plan in the
Franklin D. Roosevelt Memorial Competition, *Architectural Forum*, Feb. 1961.

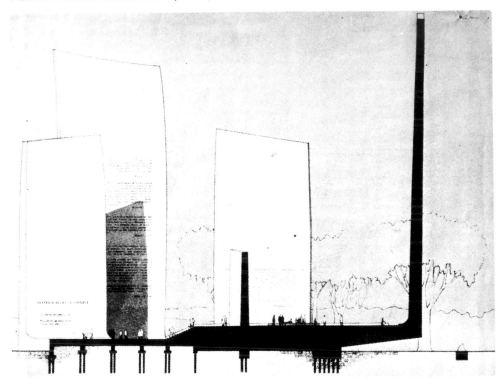

It is difficult to say which kind of monumentality is higher in quality; in my opinion, the attributes of the first kind of monumentality are simplicity, clarity, impenetrability, and impersonality, while those of the second kind of monumentality are complexity, light and shade, penetrability, and humanity. We may call the former "primordial monumentality" and the latter, "complex monumentality." The Seagram Building by Mies van der Rohe and the chapel at Ronchamp by Le Corbusier are marked by primordial monumentality and represent unequivocally the individualities of the two master architects. In the future, however, master architects are unlikely to appear. On the other hand, clusters of architecture marked by complex monumentality are likely to emerge in great numbers.

Fig. 1-27. The First Prize Plan in the Franklin D. Roosevelt Memorial Competition, *Architectural Forum,* Feb. 1961; photo by Lewis Checkman.

2

ELEMENTS OF EXTERIOR SPACE

Exterior space is very definitely architectural space and to design exterior space is to produce P-space or PN-space, integrating architecture with a roof, and exterior space without a roof. To this end, it is necessary to study scale, texture, planning, the hierarchy of spaces, etc. Let me describe my own experiences in these matters.

1 Scale

It is said that the human eye has a normal field of vision of about 60 degrees and that when we gaze at an object intently this field of vision is reduced to only 1 degree. According to the views of the nineteenth-century German architect H. Märtens,[1] which are explained in H. Blumenfeld's paper, "Scale in Civic Design,"[2] the human eye, looking straight ahead, has two thirds of the field of vision above the eye-level plane, with the visual angle above the eye-level plane being about 40 degrees. If part of the sky area is to be brought into the field of view, one can see a building as a whole at an angle of 27 degrees when $D/H = 2$ (D being the distance from the building to the observer and H being the height of the building).

According to the views of Werner Hegemann and Elbert Peets, in their *American Vitruvius*,[3] one "should be separated from the building by a distance equalling about twice its height, which means he should see it at an angle of 27 degrees. In this latter case the building will fill the entire field of vision of an observer who holds his head motionless. If the one observer wants to see more than just the one building, if, for instance, he wants to see this building as a part of a group, say, a civic center group, he should see it at an angle of about 18 degrees, which means he should be separated from the building by a distance equal to about three times its height." These figures are also used by Paul Zucker in his book *Town and Square*.[4] They are somewhat medieval and too static to be applied to design in this day of rapid change and movement, but the important thing is that it is possible to some extent to perceive the value of the over-all quality of exterior space by studying the cross section to ascertain simply whether such ratios as $D/H = 1, 2, 3$, etc., are actualized or not in the space that is going to be designed. If an architect is to design truly inspiring exterior space, then he must not only use these ratios but must go beyond them to make use of his intuitive creativity.

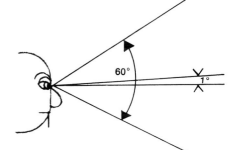

Fig. 2-1A. Field of vision.

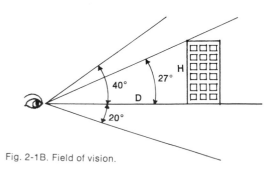

Fig. 2-1B. Field of vision.

Now we will consider the relationships between the height of buildings and the distances between neighboring buildings. If a building stands alone, it tends to become sculptural or monumental in character, with diffuse negative space surrounding it. When a new building is added to the existing developed environment, enclosing forces begin to interact with and counteract each other. According to my observation, $D/H = 1$ is the critical point at which the quality of exterior space radically changes. In other words, if D/H becomes larger than 1, we feel that the distances between buildings become rather great, while if D/H becomes smaller than 1, then we feel that the distances become rather small. When D/H becomes equal to 1, then, we feel a balance between building height and the space between buildings. In the actual laying out of buildings, $D/H = 1, 2,$ and 3 are most frequently applied, but when we exceed $D/H = 4$, the mutual interaction begins to dissipate, and the interaction between buildings is hard to perceive unless we provide some structural connections such as outdoor corridors. Conversely, if D/H is smaller than 1, the mutual interaction begins to be strengthened and we feel a sense of being closed in that builds up to a kind of claustrophobia as D/H becomes smaller and smaller. When D/H becomes smaller than 1, the form or shape of the buildings, the wall texture, the size and the location of the openings, and the angle of the light entrance into the buildings become major concerns for architects. In my opinion, when D/H is smaller than 1, a good layout is impossible to achieve unless a sufficient balance is maintained and the relationship between the buildings and the reverse space is stabilized.

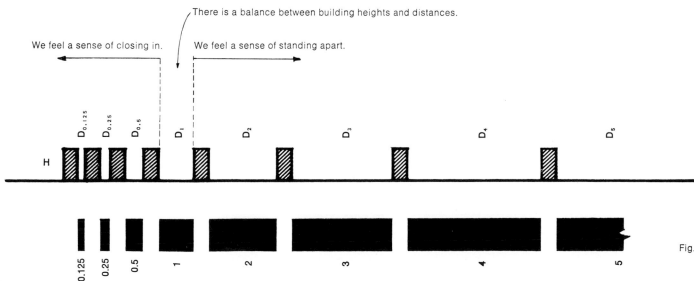

Fig. 2-2. D/H relationship in architecture.

Such relationships may be applied not only to architectural design but to human interaction. When two persons' proximity to each other lessens, the D/H ratio comes into play (H equals 8 to 12 inches). When D/H is less than 1, a very intimate interaction—intrusion space—begins. When D/H is equal to or larger than 1, the interaction is relatively normal. When D/H equals 2 or 3, that is, when the distance between faces is 2 or 3 feet, that distance is appropriate so long as two persons are conscious only of each other's face. When D/H equals 4, that is, when the distance between the faces is 4 feet, we begin to become cognizant of the upper part of the body or torso. The height of a person sitting becomes about 4 feet and a new D/H relationship comes into existence. This is expressed by $D'/H' = 1$. When two persons stand facing each other outdoors, supposing the height of the persons to be 6 feet and the distance between them to be 6 feet, the D/H ratio is again equal to 1. When the distance between the two persons becomes 12 feet, D''/H'' becomes 2; when the distance is 24 feet, D''/H'' becomes 4 and the two persons begin to lose all sense of interaction.

The above is simply an application of the architectural height-distance relationship translated into human interaction.

Now we come back to the scale of exterior space again. According to the theory of Camillo Sitte on the size of plazas,[5] the minimum dimension of a square or plaza ought to be equal to the height of the principal building in it, while its maximum dimension ought not to exceed twice that height unless the form, the purpose, and the design of the building will support greater dimensions. Translating this into the above-mentioned formulas, the width of the plaza should be represented as follows: $1 \leq D/H \leq 2$; when D/H is smaller than 1, the exterior space is no longer a plaza but a space where building interaction is too strong. When D/H exceeds 2, the enclosing forces that create the sense of plaza begin to diminish and become less operative. When D/H is somewhere between 1 and 2 the exterior space is balanced and provides a sense of proportion. The common size of the plaza as discovered a long time ago by Sitte corresponds with my own observations.

All practicing architects must be aware of the fact that exterior space should be designed on a different scale from that used for interior space. Let me formulate my hypothesis in designing exterior space on the basis of my own experience.

In the design of exterior space, a scale that is about eight to ten times that of interior space is adequate. This is my ''one tenth'' theory.

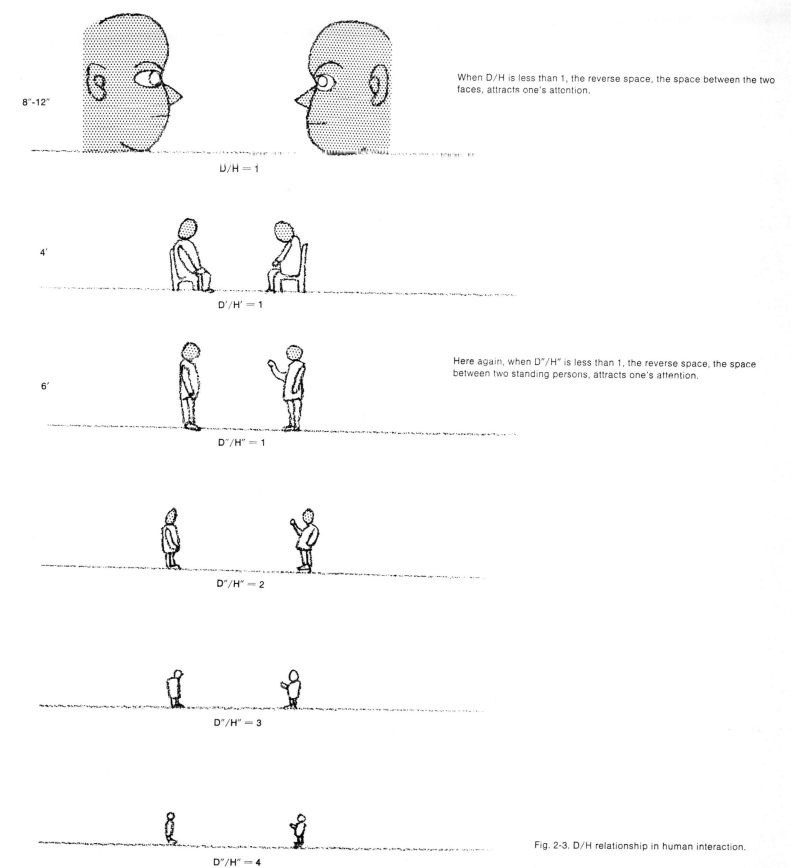

8"-12"

D/H = 1

When D/H is less than 1, the reverse space, the space between the two faces, attracts one's attention.

4'

D'/H' = 1

6'

D"/H" = 1

Here again, when D"/H" is less than 1, the reverse space, the space between two standing persons, attracts one's attention.

D"/H" = 2

D"/H" = 3

Fig. 2-3. D/H relationship in human interaction.

D"/H" = 4

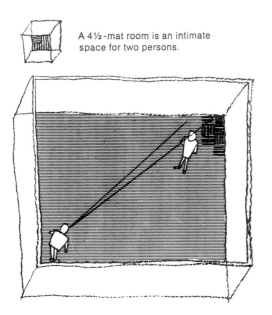

A 4½-mat room is an intimate space for two persons.

Fig. 2-4. It one attempts to create such an intimate space as a 4½-mat room (9 feet by 9 feet) outdoors, the "one-tenth" theory should be applied; that is, the exterior space should be 8 to 10 times the size of the 4½-mat room (72 to 90 feet by 72 to 90 feet).

As Edward Hall points out in *The Silent Language:* "Man has developed his territoriality to an almost unbelievable extent. Yet we treat space somewhat as we treat sex. It is there but we don't talk about it."[6] In Japan, for example, people do not name rooms for their functions, such as dining room, living room, and bedroom, but rather name them in terms of the floor space. A room of 4½ mats (one mat is about 3 by 6 feet, and 4½ mats correspond to a room 9 feet square) is small, but it provides intimate space for two persons. As the Japanese phrase, "four-and-a-half-mat novel" suggests, the mere mention of a man and a woman together in a 4½-mat room immediately conveys to the Japanese mind a very romantic situation. This is an example of the silent language in the Japanese context. If we attempt to create such an intimate space outdoors, then the above-mentioned one-tenth theory could be applied, that is, the exterior space could be eight to ten times the size of the 4½-mat room, or 72 to 90 feet by 72 to 90 feet. A space of this size is large enough for every person in it to distinguish the face of every other person; the maximum distance between people does not exceed 70 to 80 feet, and thus people can identify each other and so this size space is fairly compact and intimate, as an exterior space.

An 80-mat room (24 by 60 feet) or a 100-mat room (30 by 60 feet) is a spacious room for banquets. A room this size has been traditionally considered in Japan as the largest possible interior space in which people can interact with each other informally and in a friendly

Fig. 2-5A. A 4½-mat room.

Fig. 2-5B. A 100-mat room.

manner without losing a sense of togetherness. If we multiply a space of this size by eight, for instance, in creating exterior space, the result will be a 192-by-480-foot space, which is possibly the largest exterior space in which we can still retain some sense of intimacy. This size roughly corresponds to the average size of large plazas in European cities (190 by 465 feet) as is mentioned in Sitte's work.[7] We need not apply the one-tenth theory so legalistically in actual practice. What we have to keep in mind is that such relationships exist between interior and exterior space and that we can design accordingly. We may, therefore, be highly flexible as long as we are aware of these relationships. We may modify the one-tenth theory all the way from a one-fifth to a one-fifteenth base principle. My own designing experience suggests that a relationship between interior and exterior space of between 1:8 and 1:10 is most valid. Needless to say, in the design of stairways that are definitely related to the function of walking, treads and risers cannot be enlarged by ten times, and so the application of this one-tenth theory is limited in this case. However, it is common knowledge among practicing architects that if one designs an outdoor stairway on the same scale as an indoor staircase, the result is a flight of steps too steep and too awkward and, as an exterior design, a failure.

It is very interesting for architects to seek a series of scales that will serve as standards for creating space whether interior or exterior. In the design of exterior space, scale tends to be vague and ambiguous; therefore, it is extremely useful in designing exterior space to have a very clear sense of a series of scales for such space.

Let me state my second hypothesis on scale, based on my own experience. *In the design of exterior space a modular unit of 70 to 80 feet is useful and appropriate; this I call the "70-foot modular unit" method.*

Exterior space, when it lacks an enclosing force, tends to appear vague or limited in impact. Therefore, if it is so designed as to have a continuum of changes in rhythm, in texture, and in floor levels every 70 or 80 feet, then the monotony will be considerably decreased and the space enlivened.

The modular unit should be neither too small nor too large. My own experience suggests that a distance of 70 to 80 feet is a practical unit of design. When a building has, for example, a wall surface extending 500 to 1,000 feet, the adjacent street tends to be monotonously inhuman. We can give exterior space a sense of rhythm by designing small gardens, by providing show windows, or by making protruding elements in the wall, that is, by making some kind of change every 70

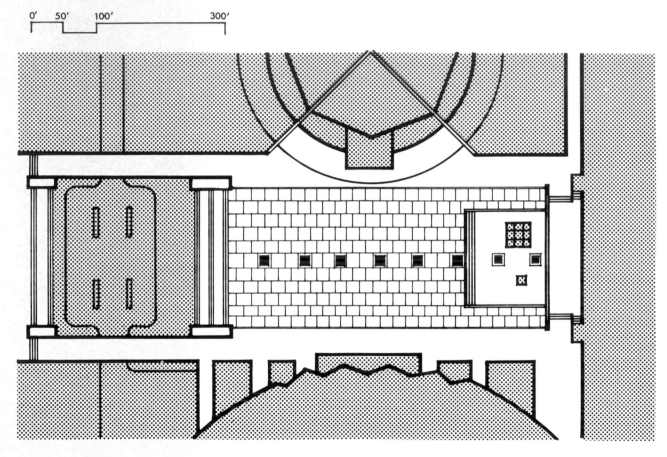

0' 50' 100' 300'

Fig. 2-6. Plan of the Komazawa Olympic Park, Tokyo.

to 80 feet. An example of this design principle is seen in Komazawa Olympic Park, in Tokyo.[8] The central plaza in this park, approximately 300 by 600 feet, is quite a large exterior space; every 70 feet or so, there are flower beds, lighting fixtures, and benches along each of the continuous axes, which extend even into the water of the ponds; thus it was attempted to bring exterior space closer to a human scale.

If we design exterior space by placing a grid composed of intervals of 70 to 80 feet over the graphic representation of the space, we can better comprehend the size and dimensions of the represented exterior space.

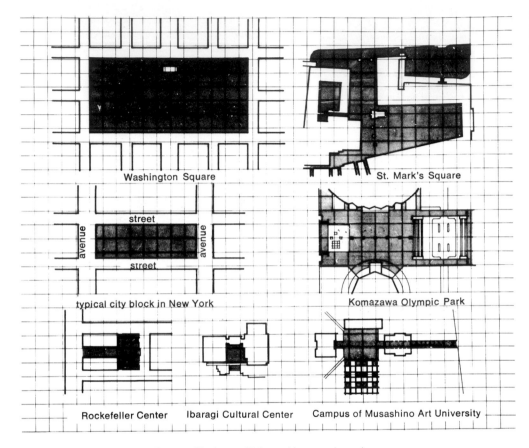

Washington Square

St. Mark's Square

typical city block in New York

Komazawa Olympic Park

Rockefeller Center   Ibaragi Cultural Center   Campus of Musashino Art University

Fig. 2-7. Placing an 80-foot grid over various plans.

2 Texture

In the design of exterior space the relationship between distance and texture is an important design element. Knowledge of how building materials appear at certain distances helps the architect to choose the materials best suited to be seen from certain distances and goes a long way toward improving the quality of exterior space.

For example, take the walls of the United Nations Building. Generally speaking, there are two kinds of walls. In one case, both the surface and the structural materials are the same, as, for example, with walls made of unfinished concrete, bricks, or stone. In the other case, the surface materials are different from the structural materials —for example, precast concrete, marble, and metal plates jointed to the structural materials. Supposing that the height of the U.N. Building is 505 feet, and that the D/H ratio is posed at 2 with the visual angle at 27 degrees, one has to be separated from the building by at least 1,000 feet to see the building as a whole. Although beautiful marble panels are jointed together on the end walls in the style of Le Corbusier, the marble revetment viewed at a distance does not always create a great visual impact, the wall surface becoming one big monolithic piece of vagueness that no longer appears to be marble. In other words, it is difficult for the viewer to determine clearly whether the building surface is an expression of the structural materials or an expression of the finishing materials. Most architects know very well that it is necessary to draw beautiful joints when designing elevations in order to enliven large, monotonous walls such as those without windows or eaves, but in practice many more devices are needed to make the actual elevations as beautiful as the drawings of them. Joints in the style of Le Corbusier in architectural drawings have become popular throughout the world, but if one is preoccupied with beauty only in drawings and does not give sufficient attention to the relationship between distance and texture, he is likely to be disappointed in the finished buildings, however good the materials he may select.

Some buildings look very fine in drawings, but the actual results leave one disappointed; on the other hand, there are buildings that do not look well on paper but are very impressive in reality. If one wants to design buildings of the latter type, he must master many varied techniques that can be learned only through experience, and so for practitioners this is a very interesting problem.

After the Second World War unfinished concrete began to become popular. The architecture of unfinished concrete has a quality of genuineness in its appearance that is lacking in buildings covered with paint or finishing materials. Even when the general public does not appreciate the quality of this unfinished-concrete architecture, some forward-looking architects have given much support to this technique. However, the experience of the past 20 years has shown that there are several problems, in terms of visual design, inherent in this type of building. One problem is that several years after completion a building tends to lose its original aliveness and the wall surface becomes dull. Also, when viewed from a certain distance, the texture created by the casting forms tends to disappear and the surface becomes a common gray wall. In order to counteract such a tendency, many architects throughout the world have begun to search for more varied textures in unfinished-concrete architecture in recent years.

Fig. 2-8. UN Building.

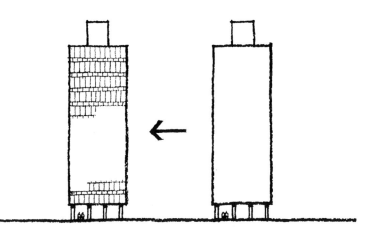

Fig. 2-9. In order to enliven large, monotonous walls without windows or eaves, most architects draw beautiful joints in the elevations. In an actual building, however, the joints are not as effective as they are in the drawings.

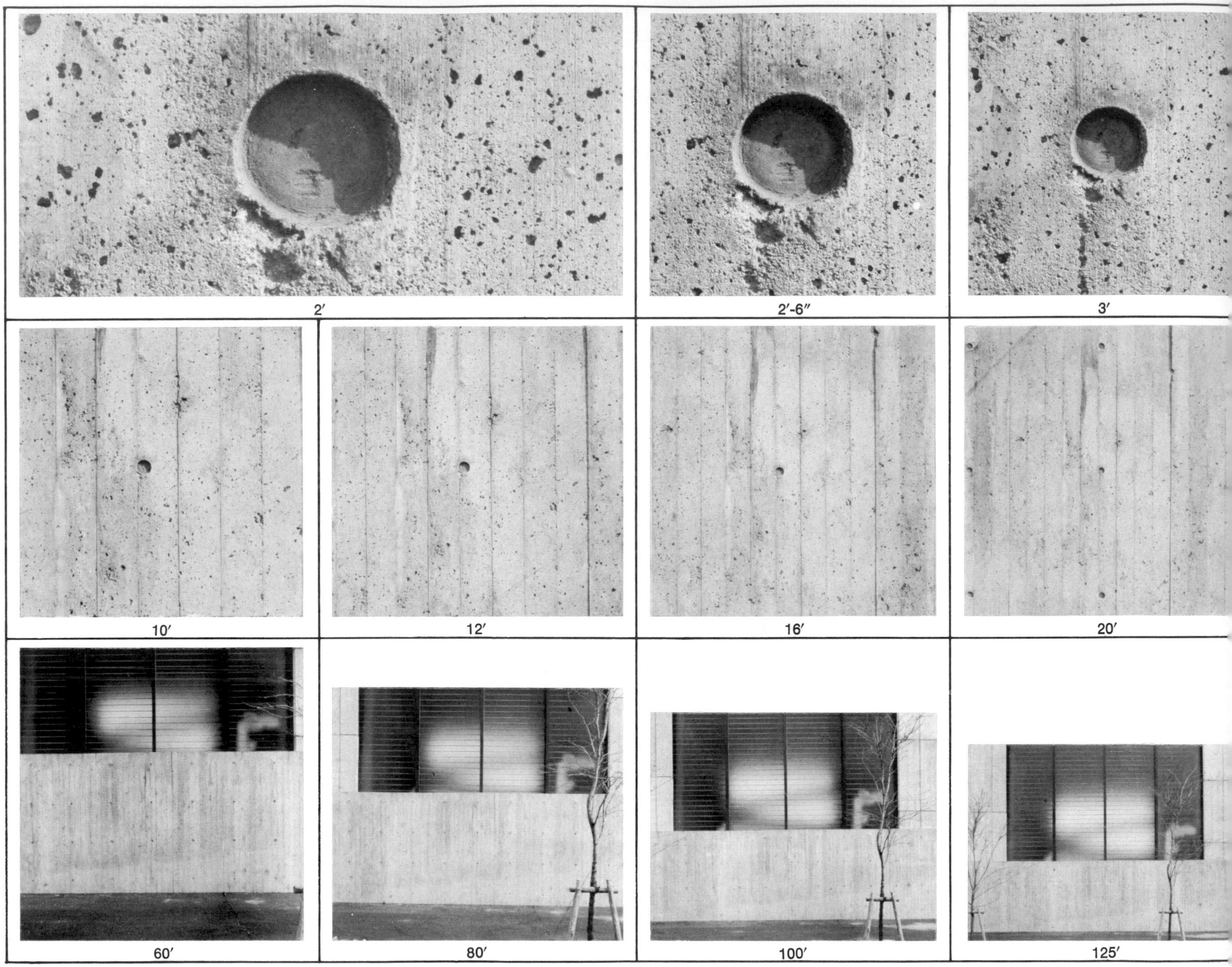
2′
2′-6″
3′
10′
12′
16′
20′
60′
80′
100′
125′

A series of photographs showing the relationship between distance and texture, Musashino Art University Library (Yoshinobu Ashihara, Arch. & Assocs.), Tokyo, Japan. (Photo by Shuji Yamada)

The photographs on pages 52-53 show the result of my experiment in which imprints of forms and form ties about 1 inch in diameter were viewed from distances beginning at 2 feet. This type of texture appears best when viewed from a distance of about 8 feet. After we

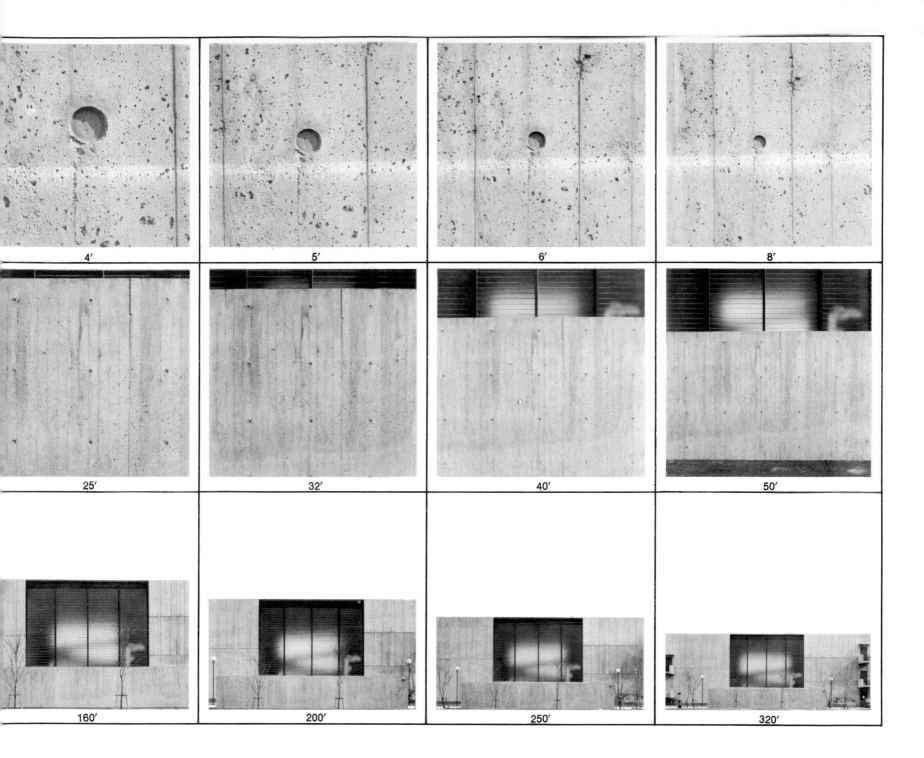

4'	5'	6'	8'
25'	32'	40'	50'
160'	200'	250'	320'

remove ourselves the distance of the modular unit, or 70 to 80 feet from the surface, the aesthetic quality of the unfinished concrete gradually tends to diminish. At 100 feet, depending on the width of the forms and the conditions of the daylight, the texture becomes al-

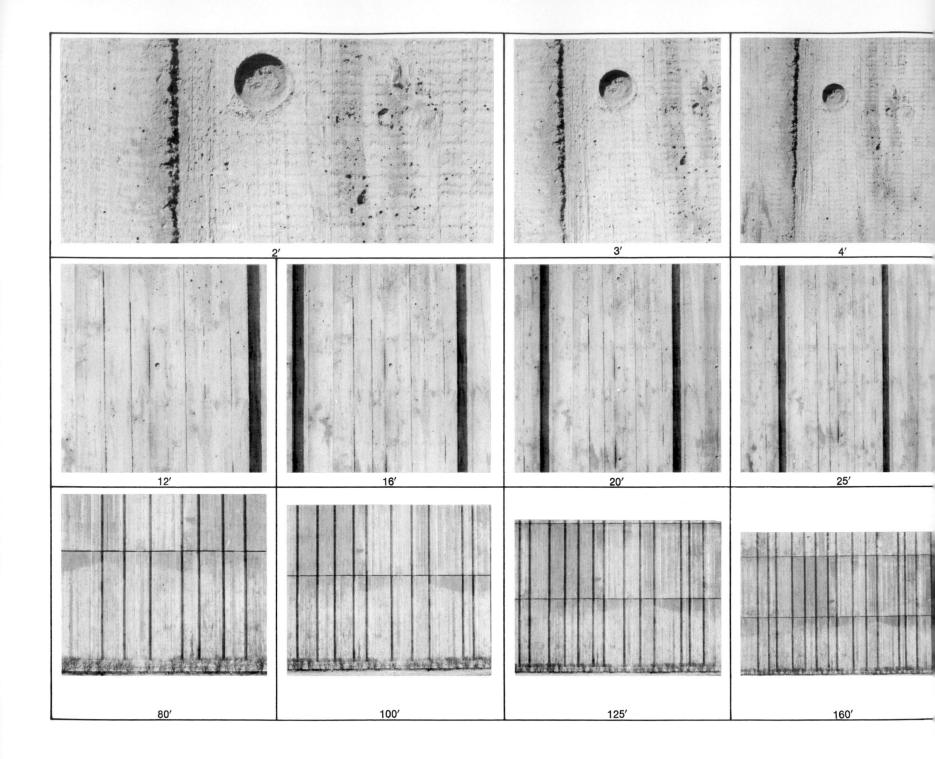

A series of photographs showing the relationship between distance and texture, Musashino Art University Library (Yoshinobu Ashihara, Arch. & Assocs.), Tokyo, Japan. (Photo by Shuji Yamada)

most invisible. At 200 feet the visibility of the texture is out of the question, and the size of the wall itself then becomes a design problem. On pages 54-55 is a series of representations at distances starting from 2 feet. At distances of up to 8 or 10 feet we can clearly see the im-

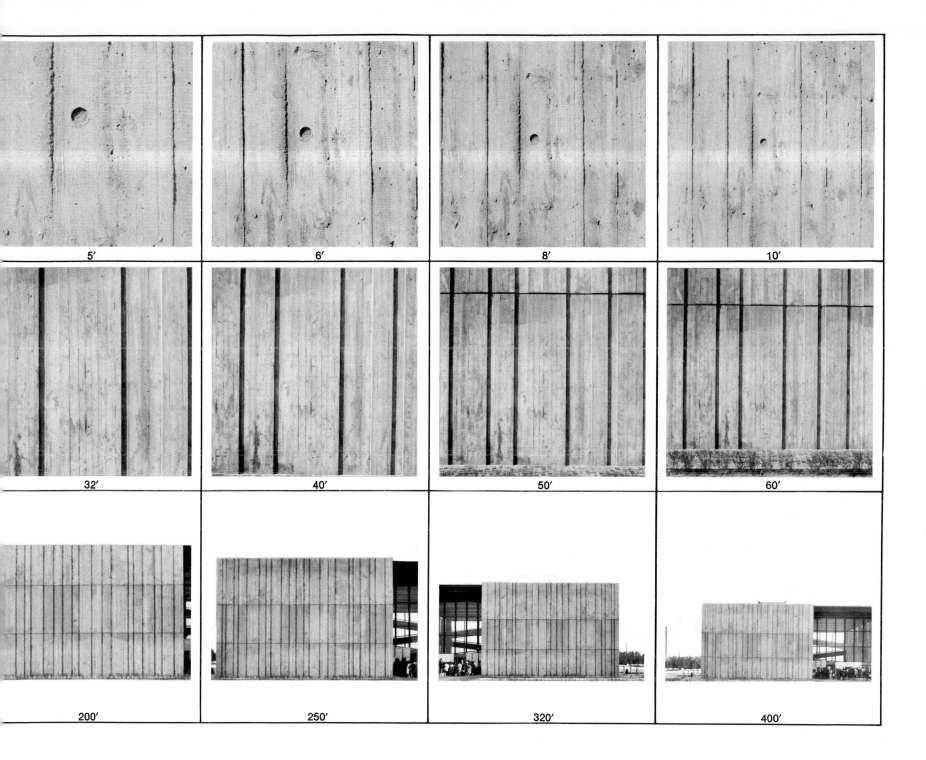

print of the forms. Beside this, the 1-inch-deep concavities imprinted at random intervals begin to attract attention when the viewer is at a distance of about 12 feet. At a distance of 70 to 80 feet, the critical point at which unfinished concrete begins to lose its texture, the verti-

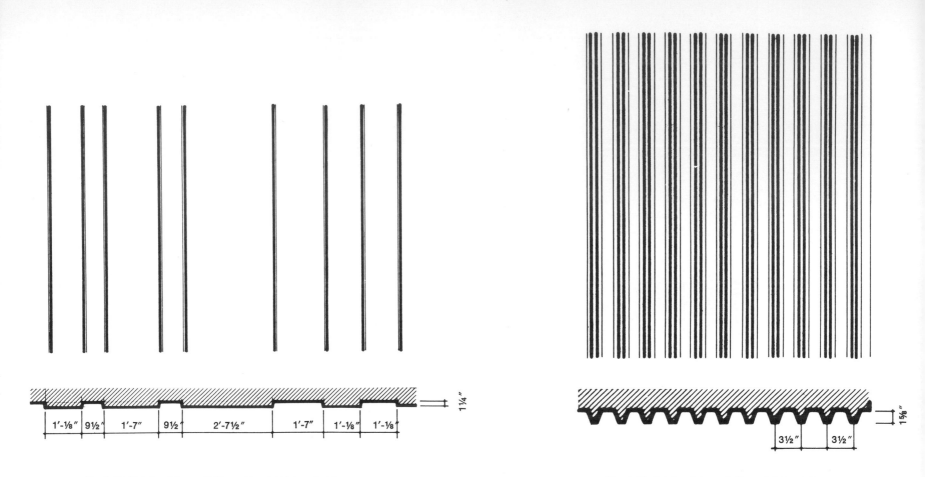

Fig. 2-10. Details of the wall, Musashino Cutural University Library.

Fig. 2-11. Details of the wall, Ibaragi Cultural Center.

cal concavities, which belong to a higher order of casting design, begin to exert a visual effect on the wall as a whole. From a distance of 160 to 200 feet the concavities located randomly become visually prominent. At a distance of 400 feet the texture created by the concavities becomes less important, and the wall as a whcle becomes centrally important.[9] The actual application of such principles is shown in the photographs. On the wall of the Ibaragi Cultural Center the pattern is created by vertical stripes imprinted in the unfinished-concrete wall surface (see photograph). The depth of these imprinted stripes is $1\frac{5}{8}$ inches. At the point where the vertical stripes and the horizontal joints meet, there are triangle sections on each end of the stripes that cast zigzag shadows and thus help to enhance the visual effect of the texture. The contrast between ordinary unfinished concrete structural members and the concave stripes imprinted on the wall surface provides a pleasing effect when viewed from any position.[10]

Fig. 2-12. Details of the wall, Iwanami Warehouse.

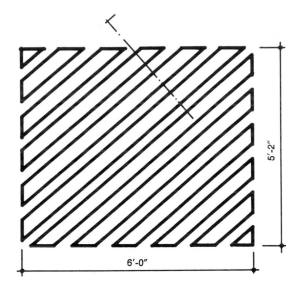

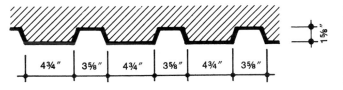

The photograph of the wall of the Iwanami Warehouse shows the herringbone pattern of concrete imprinting. As the light changes with the advancing position of the sun, the shadow patterns created by the herringbone design constantly change; this produces a contrast between shifting light and shadow areas. Compared with the wall of the Ibaragi Cultural Center, the effect is somewhat more artificial. The diagonal imprints or lines compose basic units of rectangles of about 5 by 6 feet; these units are naturally the component parts of the texture of another larger-scale order that is the "overtexture."

A 24-by-24-foot basic unit in the patterns of the paving, Komazawa Olympic Park, Tokyo, Japan. (Photo by Tomio Ohashi)

Opposite:
The overtexture of the paving, Komazawa Olympic Park, Tokyo, Japan. (Photo by Naoki Nomura)

This concept of overtexture is sometimes applied to floor design. In the central plaza of the Komazawa Olympic Park, the basic design unit is a 24-by-24-foot square, inside of which there is a diagonal line pattern that can be appreciated by the person walking in the plaza. When a person sees the plaza from a building or a high tower, the texture of the diagonal lines fades away and the arrangement of the basic design units becomes the new overtexture, thus giving the plaza a look of fullness.

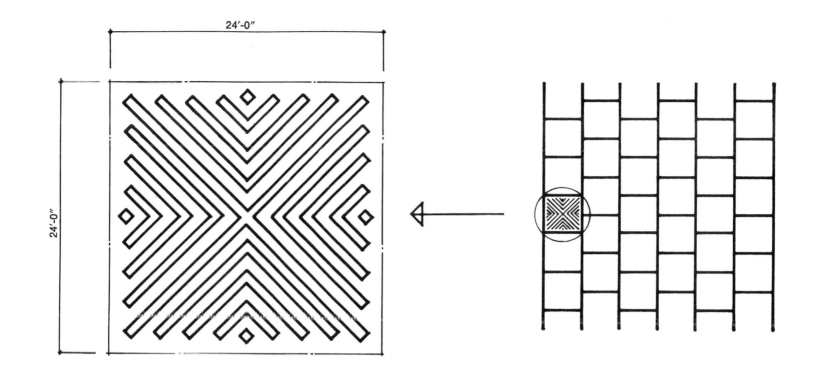

Fig. 2-13. Patterns of the paving, Komazawa Olympic Park.

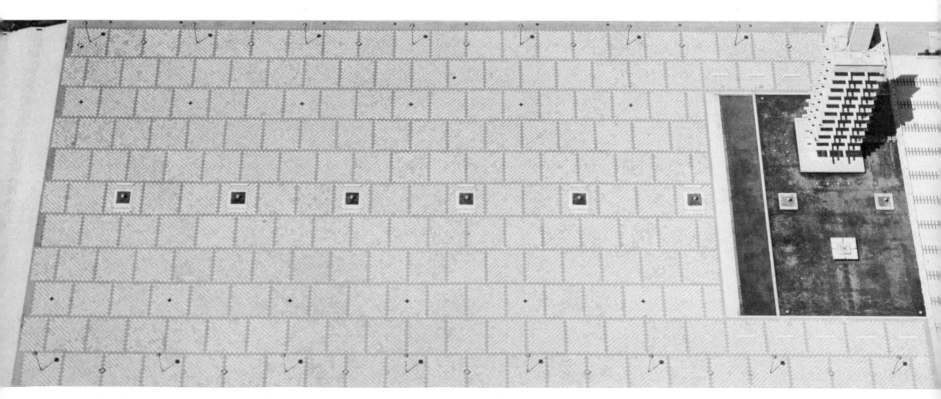

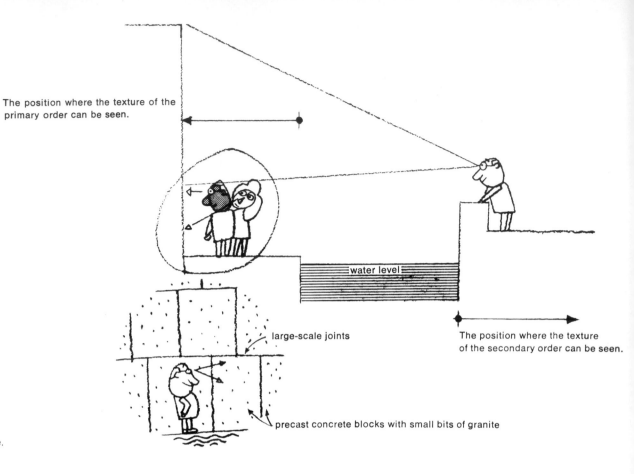

The position where the texture of the primary order can be seen.

water level

large-scale joints

The position where the texture of the secondary order can be seen.

precast concrete blocks with small bits of granite

Fig. 2-14. The primary order and secondary order in texture.

Such an overtexture method of designing exterior space could be purposely applied in many different instances. For example, when we consider the texture of a wall surface made of precast concrete blocks cast with granite aggregates, close observation reveals the aesthetic quality of this special texture; this texture is of the primary order. As we move away from the wall, the granite bits are no longer perceivable, but the joints of the precast concrete blocks become a texture of the secondary order. This hierarchy of primary and secondary textures may be deliberately designed so that exterior surfaces change in their aesthetic composition in relation to the distance from which they are viewed. If one wants to have the existence of the hierarchy of textures clearly recognized, one can achieve this effect by deliberately planning a visual discontinuity, that is, by providing some such obstacles as shrubbery and water areas so that the viewer can look only at the texture of the primary order or the texture of the secondary order, not both.

3

TECHNIQUES FOR DESIGNING EXTERIOR SPACE

1 Planning Exterior Space

If we conceive of exterior space as architecture without a roof, it is very natural that layout as a basic step in architectural design plays an important role in the designing of exterior space. The first thing for us to do is to analyze the projected uses of the exterior space and to establish the areas of this exterior space that correspond to these uses.

How shall we establish such areas? Exterior space today may be roughly divided into two basic kinds of areas: one for human beings, and one for automobiles. In order to prevent automobiles from coming into the area for human beings, one or two steps are much more effective than any traffic sign; installing small ponds and low walls is also effective. Within the area demarcated by such steps, low walls, and ponds, there can be created a visually continuous space in which human beings can behave in an unmenaced manner. To create a space in which people can move freely in any direction, as in the molecular Brownian movement, is the very first step in the planning of exterior space.

In such space for the exclusive use of human beings, man may engage in a variety of activities. This space can be roughly divided into two kinds: space for movement and space for nonmovement. Let us designate such spaces space M and space N respectively. Space M is for: 1) going to a particular destination; 2) strolling; 3) playing games or sports; 4) group or mass activities, such as parades; 5) other such activities. Space N is for: 1) relaxing, looking at the scenery, reading, waiting for friends, chatting, courting; 2) singing, discussions, speechmaking, various gatherings, ceremonies and rituals, drinking and eating, picnicking; 3) drinking fountains and public facilities such as lavatories; 4) other such activities.

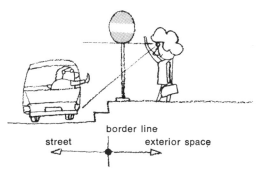

border line

street | exterior space

Fig. 3-1. One or two steps prevent automobiles from coming into an area for human beings without breaking the visual continuity of the space.

There are times when movement and nonmovement are independent of each other, and·others when they intermingle with each other. Unless space N is separated from space M, space N cannot offer the necessary sense of quietude for which it is created.

Space N must be equipped with benches, shade trees, lighting facilities, landscaping, and other such amenities. For activities such as choral singing and discussions, it is desirable also that space N be equipped with different levels, with side walls, and with rear walls.

Since the uses of the facilities mentioned in No. 3 under space N are obvious, these facilities must be designed so as not to interfere with other activities, but should be placed so that they can easily be found; planning such facilities is no different from planning indoor facilities.

On the other hand, it is desirable that space M should be flat, spacious, and without obstacles; in many cases space M functions better without any of the devices that are needed in space N.

In designing exterior space, identification of the projected uses is an important key to determining the size of the exterior space, the texture of the pavement, the form of the walls, and the height of the floors.

Fig. 3-2. For activities such as singing, discussions, and speechmaking, it is desirable for space N to be equipped with different levels, with side walls, and with rear walls.

In exterior space in which a sense of direction plays an important role, it is desirable to place a powerfully engaging object at the end of the central axis. As in Figure 3-3A, without such an object the quality of the space deteriorates toward the end of the axis, the space becomes diffused, and forcefulness is lost. On the other hand, if there is some object at the end of the axis that will attract people's attention, then the interim space becomes more forceful. For instance, in Rockefeller Center in New York the Channel Gardens are lined with shops, while at the end of the axis there is the attractive Lower Plaza, which serves as an outdoor restaurant in summer and a skating rink in winter. In the Asakusa Temple in the old section of Tokyo, the approach to the temple (83 feet wide and 970 feet long) is lined with small shops; the location of the main temple hall, the center of worship, at the end of the approach-way axis provides animation for the street, and also great pleasure to the people who enjoy shopping

Fig. 3-3.

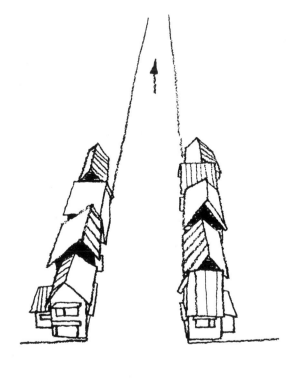

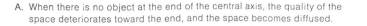

A. When there is no object at the end of the central axis, the quality of the space deteriorates toward the end, and the space becomes diffused.

B. In Rockefeller Center, the Channel Gardens lead to the Lower Plaza, which serves as a restaurant in summer and a skating rink in winter.

Rows of shops at the Asakusa Temple, Tokyo, Japan.
(Photo by Yukio Futagawa)

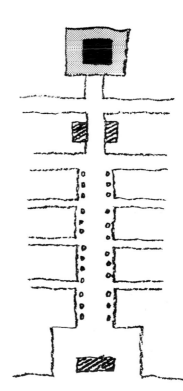

C. At the Asakusa Temple in Tokyo, an approach way lined with small shops leads to the temple hall.

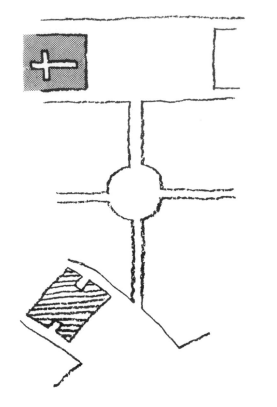

before and after worship. In the Galleria Vittorio Emanuelle II in Milan, the shopping arcade is not, in the strict sense of the word, exterior space, because it has a roof. Nevertheless, it has a charm beyond that of the ordinary shopping street because it connects the plaza of the cathedral and La Scala Theater, which are the nuclei of the city. If there is a very attractive object at the end of the exterior space then the interim space between that object and the individual becomes enlivened, and if the interim space becomes thus animated, the result is an interaction that makes the object even more forceful and attractive.

Next, let me discuss the techniques of designing exterior space, in other words, the ways of creating external order so as deliberately to permeate interior space with exterior space. Examples of such techniques are often seen in Christian churches, the concourses of railway stations, and the like. In Figure 3-4, the space enclosed by the walls looks like interior space; but since it is always open to the public, it may be said that the exterior order permeates the enclosed

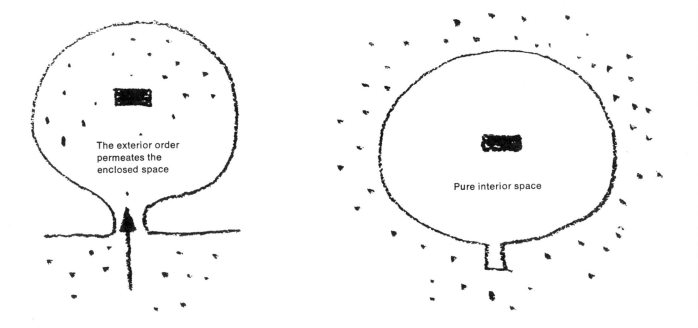

The exterior order permeates the enclosed space

Pure interior space

Fig. 3-4. The space enclosed by walls looks like interior space, but it is space permeated by the exterior order and is quite different from pure interior space.

The Galleria Vittorio Emanuelle II, Milan, Italy.
(Photo by Yukio Futagawa)

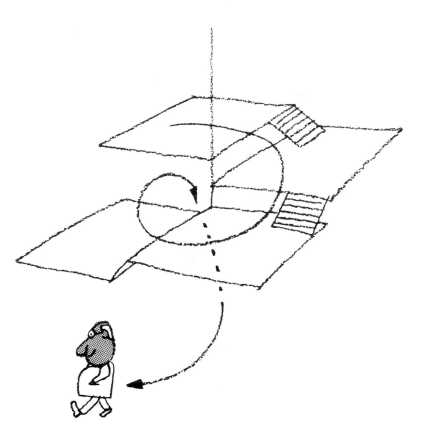

Fig. 3-5A. The showrooms in Tokyo are designed as if they were an extension of the street, with a 3-foot difference between adjacent floors.

space. Another example, in the downtown Ginza district of Tokyo, is a building for showrooms' designed above ground so that a succession of showrooms, whose floor height differs by 3 feet from adjacent floors, facilitates the permeation of interior space with features of the external order, such as the street. In this building visitors are taken to the top floor by elevator, and they walk down through a continuous row of showrooms just as if they were walking down the street. In other words, these showrooms are designed as if they were an extension of the street; the 3-foot difference between two adjacent floors is clearly indicated in the elevation shown in the photograph. Another building designed with a similar technique of permeating interior

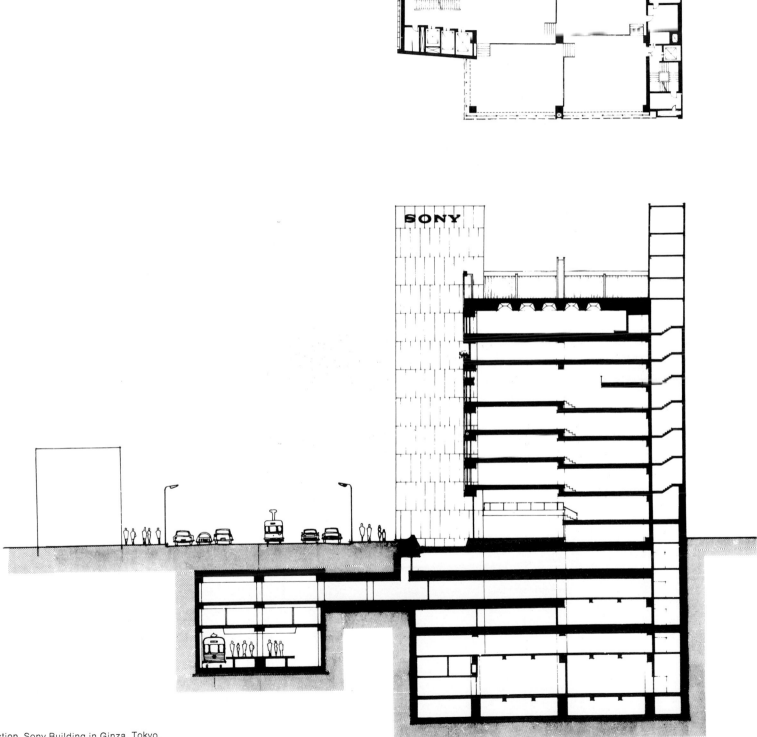

Fig. 3-5B. Plan and section, Sony Building in Ginza, Tokyo.

The differences between floors are shown in the
elevation, Sony Building (Yoshinobu Ashihara,
Arch. & Assocs.), Tokyo, Japan.
(Photo by Yukio Futagawa)

Continuous spaces inside the Sony Building, Tokyo, Japan.
(Photo by Masao Arai)

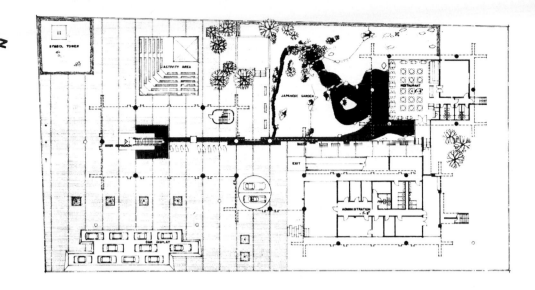

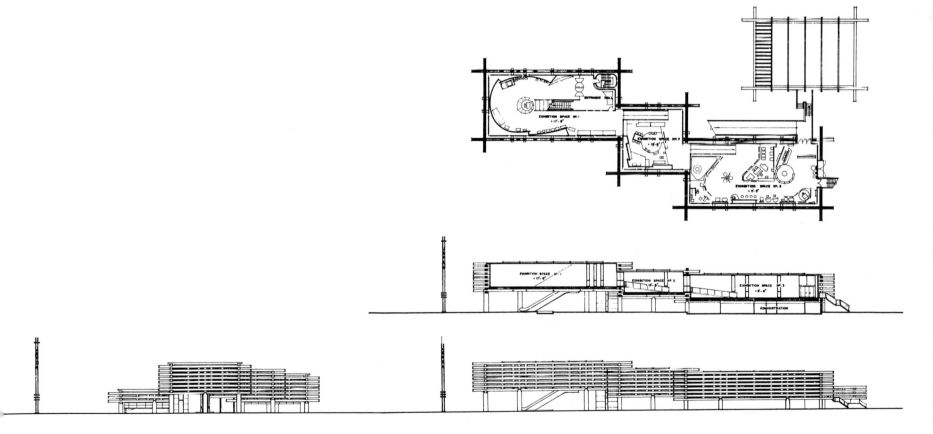

space with the external order was the Japan Pavilion at Expo 67 in Montreal,[2] where every floor differed in level from adjacent floors by 4 feet. To give one more example, there is a small provincial city library[3] designed so that the exterior order can permeate the reading rooms in order to heighten the relationship between people and

Fig. 3-6. Plans and section, Japan Pavilion, Expo 67, Montreal.

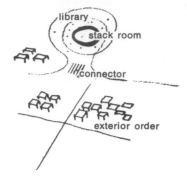

Fig. 3-7. The exterior order of a street permeates the interior space of a city library. A small plaza with a pond and an outdoor stairway serve as connectors between the street and the library.

books. The library was consciously designed so that the boundaries between the city and the library fall not at the entrance to the library but rather, since the external order permeates the interior space, around the concrete stack room. For this purpose a split-level floor was designed to give a sense of spatial continuity; a small plaza with a pond and an outdoor stairway serve as connectors between the street and the library. All of these are experiments in the permeation of interior space with the external order.

Fig. 3-7. Plan and section, Kagawa Prefectural Library.

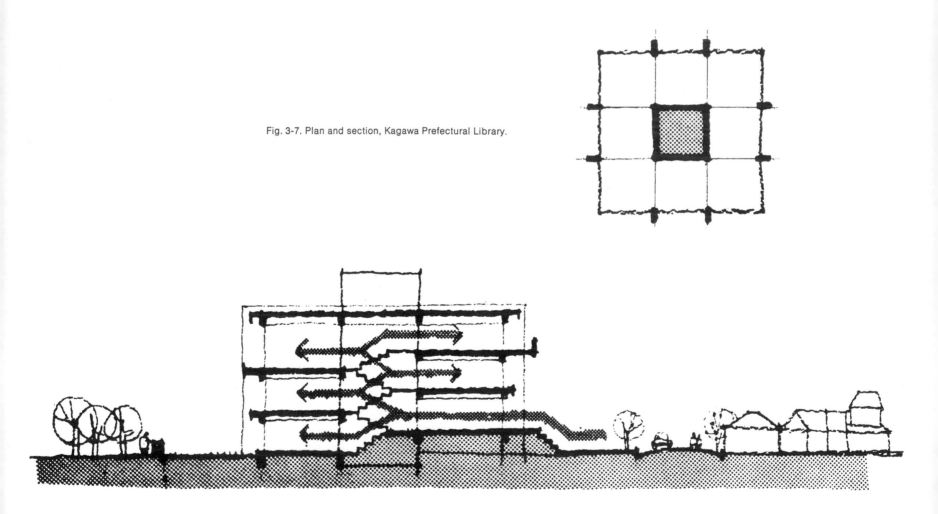

Opposite:
A connector between the library and the city, Kagawa Prefectural Library (Yoshinobu Ashihara, Arch. & Assocs.), Kagawa, Japan.
(Photo by Fumio Murasawa)

The determination of the size of the space is one of the crucial points in designing, and the analysis of the uses to which that space is to be put—even if the uses are not single purpose but are, rather, complex or vague—is important in determining the size of the space, as has been mentioned earlier. The "one-tenth theory" will be of great help in such determination. From the point of view of the visual structure of space, the size of a space should never be too small nor should it be meaninglessly large. If the modular unit in exterior space is 70 to 80 feet, one to five units will be the size most easily handled; an area of eight to ten such units will be about the maximum size within which exterior space can form a coherent whole. In planning exterior space, however, it is possible to connect several large-sized spaces with one another and somehow give order and hierarchy to the agglomeration of such spaces. This is much like building a house by combining rooms of different sizes and quality with one another by means of interior designing.

About 1,000 feet is probably the distance that a man as a pedestrian can walk with ease and pleasure; about 1,500 feet is a distance a man can walk but for which he would probably prefer to use some form of vehicular transportation if the weather is inclement; distances exceeding 1,500 feet are beyond the architectural scale in the ordinary sense of the term. It is estimated that the area that a man can feel to be his own territory lies within a circle 1,500 feet in diameter. In any case, the maximum distance at which a human being can perceive another human being will be about 4,000 feet. Exterior space exceeding one mile in length is considered too large as a townscape unless it is provided with vehicular transportation.

2 Enclosing Space

Spatial order will be created centripetally by giving some degree of an enclosed feeling to each of the component areas of the exterior space. To this end it is necessary to pay attention to the shape, quality, and location of walls.

Fig. 3-9. Enclosing space.

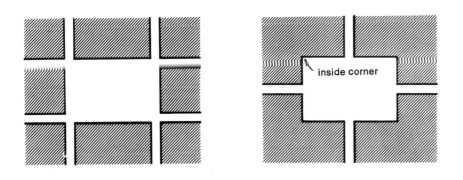

A

Fig. 3-8. The grid pattern of streets results in vertical openings at the corners, mitigating the effect of any planned enclosed feeling.

Generally speaking, a grid pattern of streets results in vertical openings at the corners of the exterior space, thus militating against the effect of a planned feeling of enclosure. It is possible, however, to enhance a sense of enclosure by providing inside corners instead of the usual outside corners of exterior space. The effectiveness of this device has already been demonstrated in the cases of the plazas of European cities.

Suppose, for example, that four round columns are erected as in Figure 3-9A: Interaction among the four columns brings into existence a space; this space is not a fully enclosed space, however, because the columns lack orientation and are diffusive. Next, suppose four walls are erected as in Figure 3-9B. Interaction among the four walls creates a space far more enclosed than that in Figure 3-9A. Further, in the case of four walls with inside right angles at the four corners, as in Figure 3-9C, the quality of the space within such walls has a somewhat greater sense of enclosure.

It is very important for architects to know how to apply the technique of enclosing space in their practice. It will be necessary to study the implications of wall height further before applying the technique.

B

C

Fig. 3-10. The significance of wall heights.

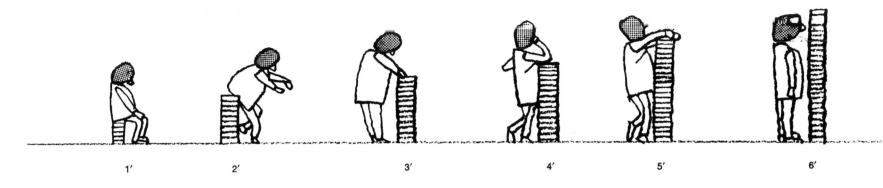

Wall height is closely related to the height of the human eye. A 1-foot-high wall has almost no enclosing force, although it can serve as a divider of areas; it also provides a place on which one can sit a little while or can place one's foot for rest. The impression created by such a wall is, at any rate, very informal. A 2-foot-high wall is not fundamentally different from the 1-foot-high wall; it provides a sense of visual continuity but has almost no enclosing force; one may be inclined to half-lean against or sit on such a wall. Further, a 3-foot-wall does not change the situation radically. When a wall becomes 4 feet high, however, it conceals the greater part of one's body, generating a sense of personal security; although it thus takes on the character of a space divider, it still provides a sense of visual continuity. When a wall becomes 5 feet high, it has some real enclosing force, concealing, perhaps, the whole body except one's head. When a wall exceeds 6 feet, it can conceal one's body almost completely and so acquires a strong enclosing force in most cases. Thus, a feeling of enclosure is obtained when a wall exceeds a man's height and breaks the visual continuity of the floor.

Low walls are primarily used as dividers of areas and do not have much to do with creating an enclosed feeling, whether they are used to form inside right-angled corners or independently to make straight walls. They are effective when used as edges along elevated floors, streams, or shrubbery.

Fig. 3-11. Low walls are mainly used as dividers of areas and do not have much to do with producing an enclosed feeling.

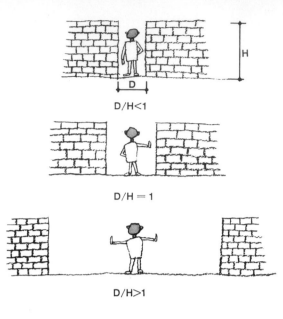

D/H<1

D/H = 1

D/H>1

Fig. 3-12. Relationship between wall heights and the width of vertical openings.

When a wall exceeds a man's height, it acquires an enclosing force, as mentioned above, and vertical openings become important. The formula concerning the building height-distance ratio, $D/H \gtreqless 1$, can be applied here. When D/H is smaller than 1 (H being wall height, and D, the width of a vertical opening), the vertical opening has the quality of an exit or an entrance, like a door tempting a man to go through it and explore the space beyond. When D/H is equal to 1, a balance is maintained. It is natural that, as D/H becomes larger than 1, the vertical opening becomes more spacious and loses the quality of a vertical opening as such, while at the same time the enclosing force of the walls diminishes.

It is thus possible to create an exterior space rich in variety by the ingenious placement of high walls, low walls, straight walls, walls with angles, curved walls, etc., with the above-mentioned facts in mind. The importance of the wall as one of the two elements that determine exterior space is well worth pondering.

3 The Hierarchy of Exterior Space

Exterior space may consist of one space, two spaces, or a number of complex spaces; in any case, it is possible to conceive of a hierarchical order in spaces.

One method of creating spatial order is to establish areas in terms of the uses and functions of the space. For example, areas can be

exterior ⟶ semiexterior (or semi-interior) ⟶ interior

public ⟶ semipublic (or semiprivate) ⟶ private

for large-sized ⟶ for medium-sized ⟶ for small-sized
groups groups groups

amusement-oriented ⟶ intermediate ⟶ quiet, artistic

sports-oriented ⟶ intermediate ⟶ nonmovement,
cultural

These are just a few possible designations of areas; in reality many different combinations are conceivable. As stated earlier, exterior space, as P-space, is, unlike N-space, full of human intentions; where there are human intentions, every kind of combination of areas is conceivable.

Fig. 3-13.

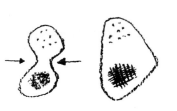

A. It is possible to conceive of a hierarchical order in a space since areas in a ???? are different in quality.

B. When two or more spaces are connected, it is natural that a hierarchical order is created.

Let me illustrate in a more concrete manner the composition of the spatial order leading from exterior through semiexterior to interior. In Figure 3-14, for example, the No. 1 exterior area is spacious, with quite a large D/H ratio, and the floor is relatively rough, with some trees planted; the No. 2 exterior space is somewhat smaller than the first exterior space, with a D/H ratio equaling 4 or 5, and the floor is paved with somewhat refined materials; the No. 3 exterior space is much smaller than the second space, with a D/H ratio equaling 1, 2, or 3, with walls possessing enclosing force, and with the floor paved with beautiful fine-grained finishing materials. As for illumination, no special lighting is needed for the first exterior space and ordinary outdoor lighting poles will do for the second, while lighting fixtures of more delicate designs are installed on the walls of the third space; thus, there are pronounced differences in illumination among the three kinds of exterior space. Outdoor fixtures, sculptures, and the like will be used to their full advantage in the No. 3 exterior space. In this way, it is possible to create a spatial order that changes from exterior to interior.

The campus of the Musashino Art University in Tokyo[5] may be cited as an example of the application of the above technique in creating a spatial sequence.

Passing through the concrete-frame gate, one enters the No. 1 exterior space, lying between the main building and the gate. This includes a brick-paved stairway and shrubbery. To reach the central plaza, which forms the No. 2 exterior space, one has to pass through the main building. All this contributes toward the formation of nodes in the exterior space. The central plaza, which has no trees but a lawn and pavement, is an enclosed space (D/H is almost equal to 4 for the width of plaza and D/H is almost equal to 5 for the length of plaza)

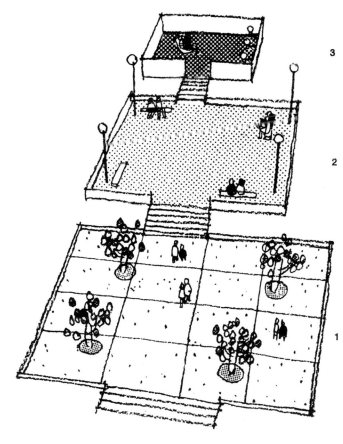

Fig. 3-14. The hierarchy of exterior space. Exterior, semiexterior, and interior spaces are connected by stairways.

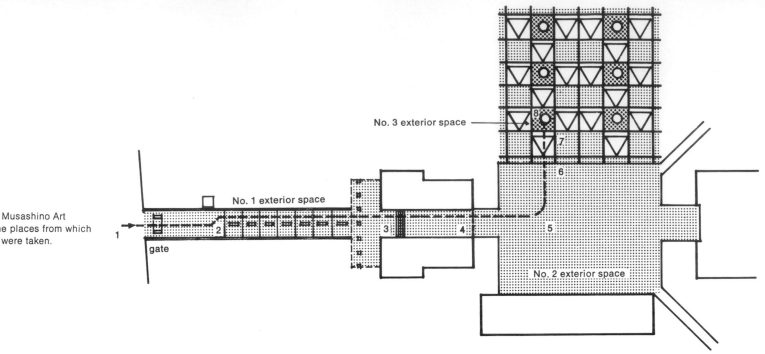

No. 3 exterior space

No. 1 exterior space

Fig. 3-15. Plot plan of Musashino Art University, showing the places from which the numbered photos were taken.

gate

No. 2 exterior space

surrounded by buildings on four sides; thus the second exterior space is, in character, far closer to interior space than is the first.

Further, on the way to the ateliers, one goes under a space supported by pilotis, climbs up a circular staircase, and then enters a small plaza (32 by 32 feet; D/H=3.5) that forms the No. 3 exterior space. This space has neither trees nor lawn; the floor is paved with clinker tiles, while wooden benches are installed against the walls. The third exterior space is an intimate exterior space with the quality of interior space, centering around the circular staircase and the lighting fixtures.

The art students thus go through three exterior spaces, with a definite spatial order, on their way to their ateliers from the busy streets; on their way back, they go through the exterior spaces in the reverse direction, from the third to the second to the first exterior space, and then they disappear into the streets. Providing nodes to tighten up space is considered very effective in accentuating the hierarchy of spaces. In the above example, the *torii*-shaped concrete gate one passes through on one's way to the first exterior space from the street, the tunnellike passage under the main building on one's way to the second exterior space, and the *piloti*-supported space one passes through going to the third exterior space are such nodes. The composition of this spatial order, proceeding from exterior through semiexterior (or semi-interior) to interior, is an attempt to stimulate the art students.

A series of photographs showing spatial order,
Musashino Art University, Tokyo, Japan.

(1) Viewing the main building through a gate.
    (Photo by Shuji Yamada)

(2) Coming to the main building.
    (Photo by Shuji Yamada)

(3) Passing through the main building to the central plaza.
(Photo by Taisuke Ogawa)

(4) Viewing the library from the main building through the plaza.
(Photo by Shuji Yamada)

(5) Coming closer to the ateliers on the left.
(Photo by Masao Arai)

(6) Going under a space supported by pilotis.
(Photo by Shuji Yamada)

(7) Entering a small plaza after climbing up a circular staircase. (Photo by Masao Arai)

(8) Entering into an atelier. (Photo by Masao Arai)

Opposite:
Aerial view of ateliers, Musashino Art University, Tokyo, Japan. (Photo by Masao Arai)

Another example of spatial order, one proceeding from public through semipublic (or semiprivate) to private, is a university campus planned on a slope at the foot of Mt. Fuji. The No. 1 exterior space in this instance is a public space surrounded by administration offices and covered passages; it is suitable for outdoor gatherings and ceremonies. The No. 2 exterior space is a semipublic space surrounded by classroom wings where students can chat with friends, read, and walk while not attending class. The No. 3 exterior space is an informal space surrounded by a dining hall, a student lounge, and a library; here students may engage in a variety of activities such as playing the guitar, singing, chatting, and even barbecuing. The three kinds of exterior space with such a spatial order are so located as to take advantage of a natural slope, with stairways serving as connectors between the spaces, which are on different levels. The finish on the ground surface, the shrubbery, the outdoor lighting fixtures, etc., are all differently designed to meet the different purposes of the public, semipublic, and private spaces. This is much like designing a guest room, a living room, and a bedroom to form the spatial order of a residence.

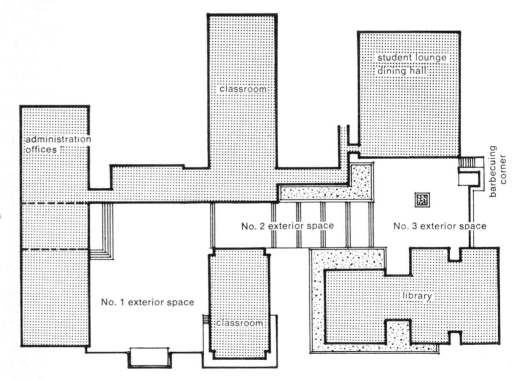

Fig. 3-16. Plot plan of a project for a university campus at the foot of Mt. Fuji (Yoshinobu Ashihara, Arch. & Assocs.), Fujinomiya, Japan.

Opposite:
A project for the university campus.
(Photo by Shuji Yamada)

An exterior space surrounded by walls carved into a slope
(Yoshinobu Ashihara, Arch. & Assocs.), Hakone, Japan.
(Photo by Yoshinobu Ashihara)

A slope may be carved out to make exterior space surrounded by walls.

Fig. 3-17

Quiet and artistic exterior space.

In creating a spatial order that proceeds from a large-sized group through a medium-sized group to a small-sized group, the "one-tenth theory" may be applied with great ease. It is possible to accentuate the spatial order by increasing the height of the walls as the scale of the space becomes smaller.

We may design an amusement-oriented exterior space for a large crowd, and also a quiet and artistic exterior space; we may design exterior space surrounded by walls carved into a slope, and a pleasing exterior space facing streams and ponds backed by walls. The important thing is to take into full consideration and make the best use of every topographical condition in creating an exterior space that is as rich in variety as the functions and nuances demanded by that space, and that is at the same time orderly.

4 The Sequence of Exterior Space

Fig. 3-18. The scenery sometimes looks more beautiful and impressive when viewed between one's own legs.

It happens sometimes that scenery looks far more beautiful and impressive when viewed through the finder of a camera. It also happens that the inclusion of the eaves of buildings or the twigs and leaves of trees in the foreground of a picture gives a sense of scale and enlivens the intervening space to a far greater extent than when a picture is taken of a distant scene as a whole. In the composition of exterior space, too, it is possible to tighten up the vista and give the space a sense of variety and anticipation by framing the visual angle. One of the simplest and clearest frames, as far as I know, is the Japanese *torii.* This frame form 田 is used not only as the sign indicating the location of shrines on Japanese maps but also as a symbol of a shrine in actual exterior space. Standing in the precincts, it indicates the direction in which people should proceed as well as serving as a frame to tighten up the vista; simple in form, it also tends to take on the quality of a monument.

Objects that are sometimes visible and sometimes hidden, depending on the viewer's movement, can also give variety to space. This effect can easily be achieved by making use of a difference in ground levels, by planting trees, and by designing walls as high as eye level. The technique of making a distant view visible for an instant, concealing it for a while, and then showing it again all of a sudden, like an underplot in a novel, is a very old and frequently used method in Japanese gardening.

The technique of designing exterior space so as to have people turn at a right angle after reaching an obstruction like a wall makes a distant view invisible and provides a sense of profundity. Changing by 90 degrees the direction in which people are proceeding can give them a completely different vista, break the spatial monotony, and provide rhythm and variety in space. This is another of the traditional Japanese techniques for designing exterior space, often applied in designing approach ways to important structures or shrines. It is easy to apply this technique to the composition of exterior space in modern architecture. It is also possible to provide still more variety for space by making ingenious use of the inside corners and outside corners that result from an application of the technique.

A close examination of the arrangements of steppingstones in Japanese gardens suggests that they are like musical scores written on the ground. Those steppingstones on which a man can walk quickly are *allegro,* while those on which a man leisurely strolls are *andante cantabile.* There are always some landmarks that suggest a change in tempo and direction, such as lanterns, and some big stones that are placed, like rests, at strategic places for people to take in the scenery. People can follow the musical scores written on the ground and appreciate the intentions of the designers of the gardens (who here correspond to composers of music), experiencing space through their own bodily movement. This is a wonderful technique of designing exterior space.

The difference between the Western and the Japanese techniques of designing exterior space often lies in whether the whole view is revealed at the very outset or gradually, step by step. It is impossible to decide which technique is better; the wisest thing for us to do is to choose one technique over the other as the occasion demands. For example, one of the best resort inns in Japan is built on a slope; when a person stands in front of the inn, he sees only the entrance of what seems to be a modest one-story building with beautifully designed horizontal lines. Upon entering the building, however, he cannot help but be impressed by a succession of spatial feats. On the other hand, the architecture of a certain hotel in Moscow is so plush that from outside it looks like a great cathedral with a pinnacle, but as a person explores inside the hotel, his initial sense of grandeur, obtained from the outward appearance, diminishes gradually.

In the design of exterior space, one effective technique is to expose the whole view at the very outset and thereby make a strong impression on people; another equally effective technique is to design exterior space so as to show it gradually, thus arousing a sense of anticipation in people and making them comprehend the whole space step by step. Is it not the highest ideal of the architect to strive to create truly inspiring, never boring exterior space by combining both techniques?

A hotel in Moscow.

A traditional Japanese inn.

Fig. 3-19

Giving a sense of anticipation by framing the visual angle, Katsura Detached Palace, Kyoto, Japan. (Photo by Yukio Futagawa)

Below and opposite:
Musical-score-like arrangements of steppingstones,
Katsura Detached Palace, Kyoto, Japan.
(Photo by Yukio Futagawa)

Japanese designers could never conceive of exposing huge structures like the pyramids to nature. They might have guided people to walls, made them turn at a right angle, led them to water, and then, all of a sudden, shown them a small pyramid. It is indeed difficult to conclude which pyramid looks larger, psychologically speaking, a huge pyramid viewed against a vast expanse of space or a relatively small pyramid seen just after one has emerged from a narrow space.

5 Some Other Techniques

There are several other points that the architect has to keep in mind when designing exterior space.

The first concerns the effective use of a difference in ground level, which makes it possible to create, for instance, an upper level, a lower level, and an intermediate level between the two. Hence, it is a very desirable technique. To vary ground levels is to designate clear boundaries between areas; the difference in ground level allows for freedom in connecting several spaces with one another or in dividing them. A sunken garden acquires an enclosing force similar to that created when walls are erected on four sides; when viewed from above, the whole space of a sunken garden can be comprehended at a glance. The sunken garden is, therefore, an effective device in designing exterior space. It may be applied in designing a large or complex exterior space, in designing an exterior space in the congested city center where the comprehension of the total space is difficult, and in designing an exterior space where it is necessary to separate people with tickets from those without tickets and yet keep both of them in the same visually continuous space.

Sunken Garden of Komazawa Olympic Gymnasium
(Yoshinobu Ashihara, Arch. & Assocs.), Tokyo, Japan.
(Photo by Taisuke Ogawa)

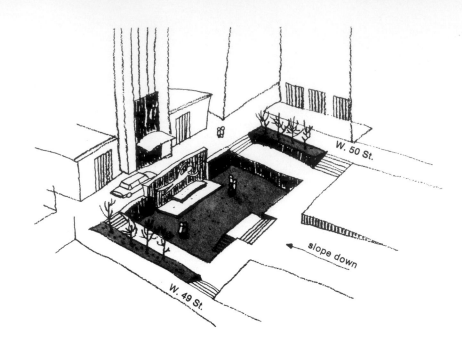

Fig. 3-20. Perspective of Rockefeller Center. The incline of the Channel Gardens makes the plaza lower than the streets; thus, the space's enclosed feeling is enhanced.

W. 50 St.

slope down

W. 49 St.

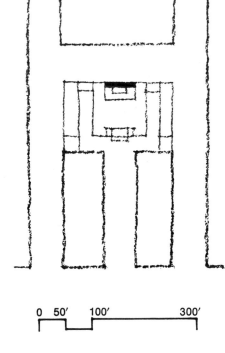

0 50' 100' 300'

Fig. 3-21. Plan of Rockefeller Center.

Rockefeller Center and Washington Square in New York are almost classic examples of exterior spaces well known not only to New Yorkers but also to tourists from throughout the world. Whereas Rockefeller Center has a three-dimensional plan based on a unified architectural plan, making use of the differences in ground level, Washington Square has a two-dimensional plan whose size has been determined by the street plan and, more especially, by the surrounding buildings, which determine the enclosed feeling, have developed spontaneously and so are disorderly. The Channel Gardens in Rockefeller Center, which meet Fifth Avenue at a right angle and extend toward the RCA Building (70 stories and 850 feet high), are 57 feet wide and 201 feet long; they are flanked by La Maison Francaise and the British Empire Building, both of which are five stories high in front and seven stories high in the setback. With a D/H ratio of about 0.7, the space in the Channel Gardens gives an impression of being enclosed, but since the soaring height of the RCA Building has nothing to do with the vanishing points of the eaves of the two buildings lining the Channel Gardens, this space, with its D/H ratio of 0.7, functions like the sliding part of a telescope and makes the vision focus forward and anticipate something as one moves toward the RCA Building. As one proceeds through the Channel Gardens, the RCA Building isolates itself clearly from the buildings on both sides; when one moves toward the center of the Channel Gardens, the sculpture of Prometheus, glittering golden against the background of a dark brown granite wall, comes into view. When one moves forward still more, the Lower Plaza suddenly comes into view. As is well known, this

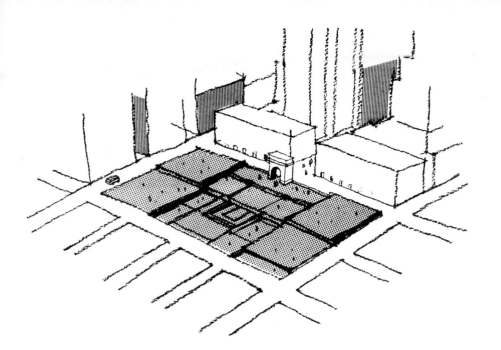

Fig. 3-22A. Washington Square, which has an area of 930 feet by 440 feet, seems to be too large. If it were divided into several plazas, each with a sufficient enclosed feeling, the square would be much improved.

Lower Plaza serves as a skating rink in winter and as an open-air restaurant in the other seasons. Those who go to the RCA Building from Fifth Avenue via West 49th Street or West 50th Street need not climb any stairway, while those who pass through the Channel Gardens on their way from Fifth Avenue to the RCA Building have to climb up one of four stairways. This is because the Channel Gardens are inclined. However, it may be said that a majority of people climb up and down the shallow stairways unconsciously, without knowing that the Channel Gardens are inclined. The incline of the Channel Gardens provides a sense of movement and orientation, while the walls formed by the four stairways surround the Lower Plaza and enhance its enclosed feeling. It has been possible to improve this enclosed feeling even on flat ground by inclining the Channel Gardens, by utilizing the subsequent differences in level, and by creating walls. As a result, factors have been produced that encourage people to stroll, rest, and view the area in a leisurely manner.

On the other hand, Washington Square is a park surrounded by streets rather than an exterior space proper. The large rectangular space (440 by 930 feet) has as vertical openings 14 streets piercing the "walls" formed by the surrounding buildings. The skyline over the square is irregular, with the D/H ratio being about 4.5 on the average, and the enclosed feeling is not very strong. If this large square had been divided into several sunken gardens, each with its own function and character, its enclosed feeling would have been considerably increased.

While on the subject of a difference in ground level, it is well to

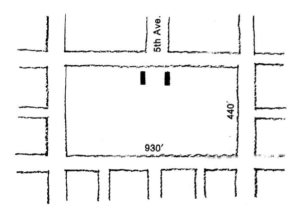

Fig. 3-22B. Plot plan and perspective, Washington Square.

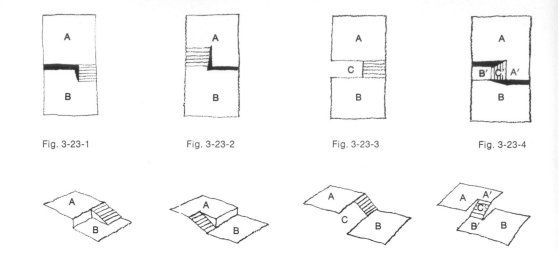

Fig. 3-23A. Different ways of connecting two spaces by a stairway.

Fig. 3-23-1   Fig. 3-23-2   Fig. 3-23-3   Fig. 3-23-4

touch on outdoor stairways and ramps that connect floors on different levels. Suppose there are two spaces, A and B, on different levels, with space A on a higher level than space B. Basically, there are three different forms of stairways and ramps to connect space A with space B: a stairway located in space B (Figure 3-23-1), a stairway located in space A (Figure 3-23-2), or a stairway located in space C, which is neither space A nor space B (Figure 3-23-3). Figure 3-23-4, in which space A extends to space A′, and space B to space B′, and in which the stairway is located in space C′, is a variation of Figure 2-23-3. Judgment as to the location of stairways and ramps, whether in space A, space B, or space C, seems very simple at first glance, but it is as important a decision as whether vertical or horizontal lines should be emphasized in drawing the elevation of a building. When space A and space B are connected by a stairway, the location of the stairway—at the end, in the middle, or along the whole of the area where the two spaces meet—will determine where functions other than walking will

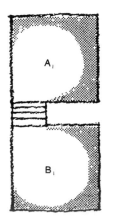
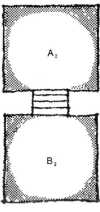
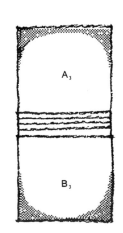

Fig. 3-23B. Functions other than walking tend to concentrate in the dotted area, away from a stairway.

be located. Thus, the decision is an important one in planning exterior space.

Stairways in exterior space should be wide enough to enable people to pass each other without touching. It is also desirable that the tread for outdoor stairways be wider and the riser lower than for indoor staircases, as mentioned earlier.

The impressions outdoor stairways make vary greatly, depending on the location and length of their landings. As Figure 3-24A shows,

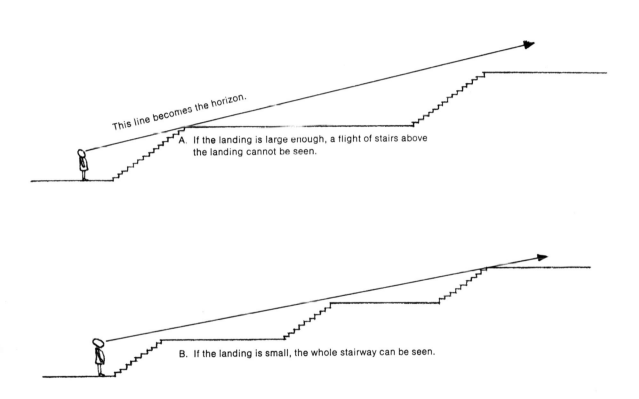

This line becomes the horizon.

A. If the landing is large enough, a flight of stairs above the landing cannot be seen.

B. If the landing is small, the whole stairway can be seen.

Fig. 3-24. Stairways and landings.

when a man stands at the foot of a stairway, he cannot see the flight of stairs above the next landing if the landing is too large; the top step of the first flight becomes a horizon for him. As he moves up the first flight, the next flight gradually comes into view; if there are a large number of landings, flights become visible one after another as the man moves up the stairway. On the other hand, if there are few landings, and if each landing is small, a man can command a view of the whole stairway at once.

1

2

The changing vistas of the control
tower of Komazawa Olympic Park
as one proceeds up the stairway.
(Photo by Shuji Yamada)

3   4

When the top step of a stairway forms a horizon and some object presents itself suddenly over this horizon, a man focuses his attention on it; then, as he moves up the stairway, the impressive object reveals itself to him little by little, literally step by step. Such a design for a stairway has been actually attempted in the Komazawa Olympic Park in Tokyo. The stairway in this park is 300 feet wide, and as shown in its section (Figure 3-25) the view of the tower ahead changes slowly as one moves up the stairway. When one reaches the upper plaza, he can suddenly command a view of the whole plaza.

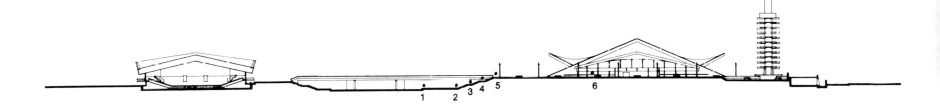

Fig. 3-25. A stairway in the Komazawa Olympic Park, showing places from which the numbered photos were taken.

5   6

One's feeling in going up a stairway is different from that in going down the stairway. Such feelings may be compared to one's psychological states in climbing up and down a mountain. It is quite common that, in climbing down a mountain a person has just conquered, he no longer retains the sense of anticipation and discovery that animated him in climbing up.

Second, edge lines formed by the meeting of two planes or formed by different materials are an important element in design. Even when the wall surface is somewhat uneven, a finished room often gives an impression of being extremely well done if the lines formed by the meeting of walls and ceiling are straight. In exterior space, which is larger and commands a better vista than interior space, special attention should be paid to such edges.

Anyone can easily notice the difference between simple and unstable tracks for trucks at construction sites and exactly parallel tracks for express trains. A quick look at tracks, even without running vehicles over them, will tell with what degree of precision the tracks have been laid. Similarly, an examination of the edges of pavements, of streets, and of plazas tells of the finish of streets and plazas as a whole. Materials used for edges must be of a higher quality than the materials used for the pavement in general.

In the composition of exterior space, an error in the arrangement of objects that should be placed at equal intervals or on a straight line detracts frequently from the quality of the exterior space. It is the same in the case of lines that should be exactly parallel but are not. So we should place objects as precisely as possible, especially when we use fine-grained or elaborate materials. At the same time, however, we should remember that the deliberate effort to arrange objects in a seemingly random pattern is sometimes very effective, particularly when we use rough and unfinished materials.

Granite edges in brick pavement, Ibaragi Cultural Center.
(Photo by Masao Arai)

Ibaragi Cultural Center.
(Photo by Shigeo Okamoto)

Opposite:
Granite edges in brick pavement,
Okayama Children's Center
(Yoshinobu Ashihara, Arch. & Assocs.),
Okayama, Japan.
(Photo by Yukio Futagawa)

Variety of pavement. Clubhouse of N.Y.K. Lines
(Yoshinobu Ashihara, Arch. & Assocs.), Tokyo, Japan.
(Photo by Masao Arai)

Third, water does not perhaps play a significant role in regions with a severe climate, but in temperate regions water is an important factor in creating exterior space. Water uses may be divided into two general kinds: still and flowing water systems. Still water can give space an indescribable depth by reflecting objects, and illumination at night can multiply the aesthetic effect of such reflections. Flowing water is provided by streams and fountains: When used at a low level, it is extremely useful in establishing spatial boundaries and at the same time in maintaining a visual continuity of space. Placing water gates at several places may help accentuate the movement of the water.

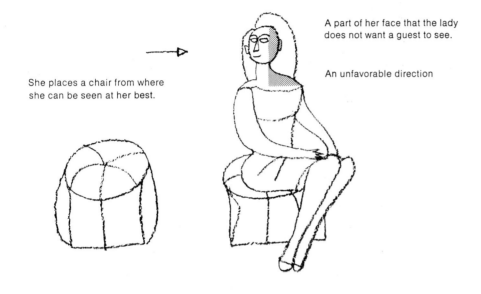

She places a chair from where she can be seen at her best.

A part of her face that the lady does not want a guest to see.

An unfavorable direction

Fig. 3-26. When there is a certain direction from which she can be seen favorably, a lady guides her guest to the place from which she can be seen at her best. This principle can be applied to exterior design.

One effective use of water is as a barrier to areas people are not to enter. Such a use may be compared with the posture a lady takes when there is a certain direction from which she can be seen unfavorably. She carefully guides her guest to the position from which she can be seen at her best. Water may similarly be used so that exterior space will not be seen from an unfavorable direction. Exterior space design is interesting to the architect since it provides him with a great degree of freedom in thus stopping and accelerating people's movements.

Lastly, let me compare two classic examples of exterior space that date back to about the same historical period; one is St. Mark's Square, in Venice, and the other is Itsukushima Shrine, about 12 miles southwest of Hiroshima. These two exterior spaces are geographically poles apart and have no historical relationship with each other, and yet one cannot help but be strongly impressed with some similarities in spatial composition between the two.

Ho-o-do reflected in the water, Uji, Japan.
(Photo by Yukio Futagawa)

St. Mark's Square, Venice, Italy. (Photo by Yukio Futagawa)

Itsukushima Shrine, Miyajima, Japan. (Photo by Yukio Futagawa)

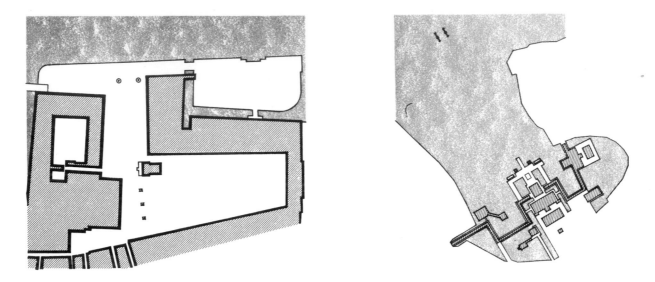

Fig. 3-27. Plot plans of St. Mark's Square and Itsukushima Shrine.

St. Mark's Square originated as the parvis of St. Mark's in the ninth century and flourished as a marketplace in the early eleventh century. Much expansion and remodeling work has since been undertaken, mostly in the sixteenth and seventeenth centuries, centering around St. Mark's Cathedral itself.[5] Since the formation of the exterior space in this plaza has taken so many years, no two buildings are exactly parallel. For example, the Palace of the Doges built between 1309 and 1424 and one of the most beautiful arch buildings in the world, is not exactly parallel with Scamozzi's Library facing it; it is also considerably set back from the line of St. Mark's Cathedral. The Procuratie Vecchie and the Procuratie Nuove are not parallel either. This lack of parallel arrangement of buildings is a distinctive feature of St. Mark's Square. The most impressive thing about the plaza is, however, the view of the sea, between the walls of the Palace of the Doges and Scamozzi's Library, from the Piazzetta, into which one enters after turning at a right angle from the plaza in front of St. Mark's Cathedral. Two granite columns, one the Lion's Column (1189) and the other the Column of St. Theodore (1329) with the sea as background, tighten up and punctuate the space in the Piazzetta. This is the place where no visitor to St. Mark's Square fails to take a picture.

Itsukushima Shrine is a historical shrine, part of which is submerged in sea water. Its origin dates back before the ninth century; in the eleventh century the shrine was burned down twice, and the big *torii* in the sea has been damaged by typhoons and thunderbolts and has had to be rebuilt several times.[6] The façade of the shrine faces the northwest; the main hall is located in the southeast, near the beach; in front of the main hall is a rectangular hall of prayer; farther on, in front of the hall of prayer, is a rectangular purification hall. The wood-floored, roofless area in front of the purification hall is a low dancing platform whose central part, elevated three steps, forms a high dancing platform surrounded by handrails. This extends toward the east and west on the northern side of the high dancing platform, with musicians' rooms and shrines to right and left; it narrows down in the center toward the north, and at the end of the long narrow area there is placed a bronze lantern dating back to the Edo period. Farther to the north (510 feet), in the sea, is located the big *torii.* The view of the lantern and the *torii* over the high dancing platform against the background of the sea is beyond description—it provides a seascape no less impressive than does St. Mark's Square. Here sacred dances and festivals have been performed since ancient times, and even today various festivals are held several times a year, attracting national interest.

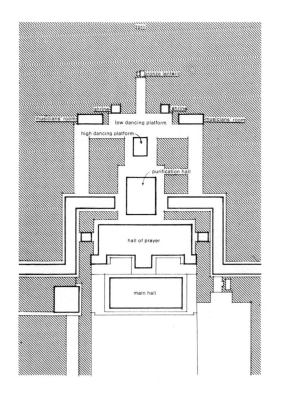

Fig. 3-28. Plan of Itsukushima Shrine.

Both St. Mark's Square and Itsukushima Shrine date back to the ninth century, and both have undergone much change and renewal in their long development to the present day. Both accommodate definite religious functions, attracting large crowds of people on various occasions. A comparison of the picture of a parade at St. Mark's Square, drawn by Gentile Bellini in the late fifteenth century, and the pictures of activities at Itsukushima Shrine collected in the *Itsukushima Picture Scroll* show how the two exterior spaces were each useful in fulfilling the functions for which they were originally de-

Fig. 3-29. Picture of a parade in St. Mark's Square by Gentile Bellini, plate 34, below, from *Town and Square* by Paul Zucker. Courtesy of Columbia University Press.

signed. The areas where the sea is visible and the areas where the
sea is not visible are in both cases ingeniously connected; in the
areas where the vistas open up toward the sea, the two granite columns are placed in St. Mark's Square and the bronze lantern and the
big *torii* are placed at Itsukushima, the objects in both serving to
tighten up the space. It is interesting to note that this technique of
viewing the seascape at its best was developed at about the same
time, many centuries ago, at two such different places separated by
so many thousands of miles.

Fig. 3-30. Picture of activities at Itsukushima Shrine, in *The Itsukushima Picture Scroll*. Courtesy of Kodansha Publishing Co.

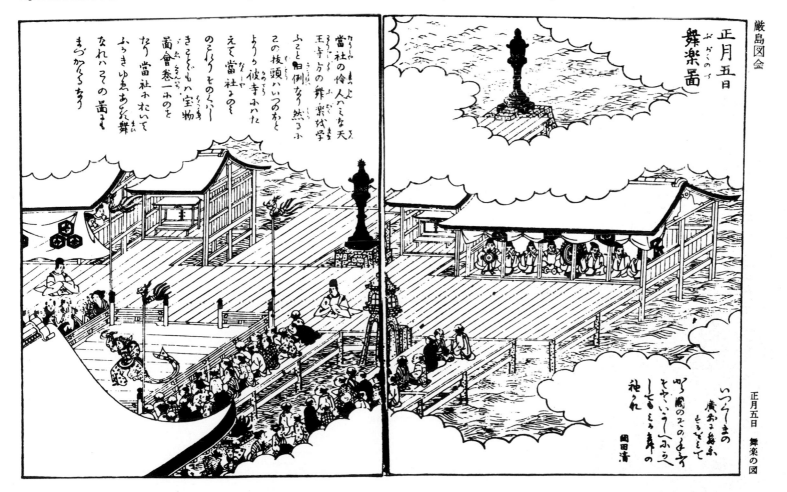

4

THE CREATION OF SPATIAL ORDER

1 Space Created by Addition
and
Space Created by Subtraction

Necessary materials are added.

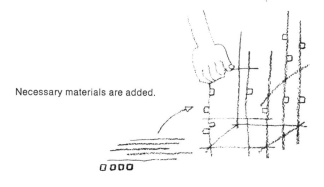

Space created by addition.

Unnecessary parts of materials are removed.

Space created by subtraction.

Fig. 4-1.

Just as there are two ways of sculpting, one by adding something to the existing material and the other by carving out unnecessary parts from the existing material—such as masses of stone and wood—there are two ways of creating space, one by building architecture centrifugally, from the inside to the outside, and the other by building architecture centripetally from the outside to the inside. In the former, the inside is first determined, and then the creation of order proceeds from the inside to the outside; parts are assembled, multiplied, and expanded step by step into an organic whole after the internal functions and space have been thoroughly studied, even if the result is to the detriment of the outside. Although each part is thus very human and can well be designed, the over-all structure is sometimes confusing when it exceeds a certain size. In the latter way, the outside is first determined and the creation of order then proceeds from the outside to the inside; the over-all structure is analyzed, fragmented, and built inward in accordance with a certain system after the scale of the over-all structure and the systematic arrangement of interior space have been thoroughly studied in relation to the scale of the city, even to the detriment of the insider. Here, although each part is uniformly treated, sometimes even to the extent of causing inconvenience to those who use the building, the over-all structure is likely to be well-balanced, logical, and orderly.

Two different ways of creating spatial order suggest themselves if we compare the works of the Finnish architect Alvar Aalto and the French-Swiss architect Le Corbusier. In the plans of some buildings designed by Aalto, there are asymmetrical auditoriums, sometimes puzzling zigzag forms, wall lines that meet each other at acute or obtuse angles, and freewheeling curves; as a result, in the elevations of these buildings there are also zigzag eaves and unexpected curved planes. Aalto's works seem to have contradictions to persons who have not seen them at first hand but have attempted to judge them on the basis of plans alone. On personal observation, however, people are captivated with the inscrutable charm of his buildings. The zigzag forms, for instance, which look puzzling in the drawings, come to life and give fantastic nuances to the buildings; the eaves, staggered like a flight of wild geese, reduce monotony and achieve an aesthetic effect against the background of needle-leaf trees. It is now clear that the front and back walls, which are not parallel in plans, create no problems at all. The plans exist only in theory; once the walls emerge as actual space dividers in architectural space, the fronts and backs of walls form spaces independent of each other, with no visual connection. Thus Aalto's magic impresses people with the beauty of each independent space. The well-designed door hardware, the handrails of the staircases, the lighting fixtures, the furniture, and the carpets are also placed with great care, leading persons moving around in such a space to feel its wonder with their own senses. It seems that Aalto has carefully made use of the fact that the individual does not experience simultaneously the two spaces divided by a wall, so the architect may add more and more space as need arises.

In contradistinction to the creation of the spatial order from in to out, or space made by addition, is the creation of the spatial order from out to in, or space made by subtraction. What, then, is architecture by subtraction like? Le Corbusier's works seem to me to be examples of this architecture. Let us examine his Unité d'Habitation in Marseilles. The building looks so sculptural that the viewer is almost deluded into thinking that a master sculptor has carved dwelling

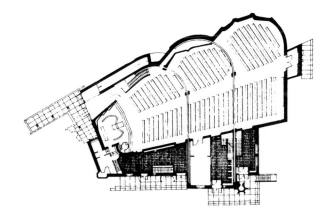

Fig. 4-2A. Church at Vuoksenniska, Finland, by Alvar Aalto.

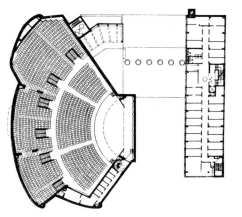

Fig. 4-2B. Plan of Kultuuritalo, Helsinki, Finland, by Alvar Aalto.

Otaniemi Technical College (Alvar Aalto),
Otaniemi, Finland.
(Photo by Yukio Futagawa)

Door hardware,
Otaniemi Technical College.
(Photo by Yukio Futagawa)

Apartment house (Le Corbusier), Marseilles, France   (Photo by Yukio Futagawa)

units into this mass of concrete with a chisel. When one enters one of the apartments, the suspicion flashes through his mind that the elongated room so famous among architects has been designed to contribute toward a better proportion of the huge building rather than to provide a man with good living conditions. It may be, however, that the ingenious arrangement of living units and the impressive orderly elevation, with its deep concavities, compensate for the deliberate disregard of the functions of the interior space. Here, heart-warming details, such as the door hardware of Aalto's works, are difficult to find. It may be, however, that such matters can safely be ignored in view of the grandeur of Le Corbusier's over-all architectural conception.

By thus comparing the works of the two master architects from the point of view of my space theory, I merely point out that these two opposite approaches to architecture exist. It is inconceivable that Aalto could have designed such narrow dwelling units as Le Corbusier did in the Marseilles apartment house. Architecture creating order from the outside to the inside tends to be self-conclusive, sculptural, and monumental. In this sense, Le Corbusier's works are very positive architecture. On the other hand, Aalto's works can be examples of creating order from the inside to the outside, and so they can accommodate natural expansion and cope with changes in internal functions with ease.

It may be said that Aalto is an architect whose works, to be truly appreciated, are best seen at first hand against the background of the Finnish landscape rather than in photographs, while Le Corbusier is an architect whose architectural thinking has such a universality, transcending all local environments and provinciality, that comprehension of his theory is as impressive as seeing his architecture at first hand. This is amply demonstrated by the facts that only the limited number of people who have seen Aalto's architecture in person have become his ardent admirers, and that he is a kind of national hero in Finland; on the other hand, Le Corbusier is admired by architects and young architecture students all over the world who have not personally seen any examples of his work, whereas he was rather coldly received in France, his adopted country.

Space created by addition has a certain limit in scale beyond which additions result in a "hardening of arteries," and, finally, in chaos. It is, therefore, not desirable that space created by addition grow beyond that limit. In large, complex projects, it is, however, possible to employ both methods of creating order and so enhance the quality of the space through the influence of the two approaches on each other.

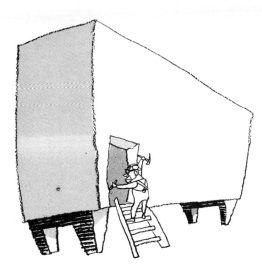

Fig. 4-3. The Unité d'Habitation in Marseilles looks like a big piece of sculpture carved by a master sculptor with a chisel.

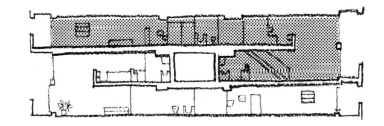

Fig. 4-4. Section of the Marseilles apartment house by Le Corbusier.

2 Internal Order and External Order

In the city man cannot live alone like Robinson Crusoe. This is because the essence of urban life is the division of labor, and the more advanced the urbanization, the more specialized the role each individual plays in his social life. Thus, the citizen of a large metropolis does not know at all what kind of contribution he is making toward the functioning of social organization; he fights a mounting feeling of alienation on the one hand and attempts to live, work, and play collectively in the high-density urban space on the other.

As the division of labor and specialization advances, co-ordination and synthesis are required; especially in a complex society like today's, we have to achieve social efficiency through the division of labor and synthesis. To this end, it is necessary to provide adequate means of transportation and distribution, and the channels for moving energy and information. When the degree of division of labor and specialization in architecture is low, there is no serious problem even if buildings are small and isolated; when, however, specialization in architecture advances, it becomes imperative that buildings be clustered and well co-ordinated with one another. A cluster of architecture is not merely the sum total of individual buildings; it can—and should—be an efficiently co-ordinated and internalized group of buildings.

Suppose, for example, an extremely simple building for a cottage industry (Figure 4-5A). Outside the building there is N-space, while inside it there is productive space allocated for storing the raw materials and for assembling and storing the finished products, and also living space for those who do the work. When these spaces are rationally located inside the building, "interiors" for the cottage industry come into existence and "an internal order" that satisfies a function is created.

When, however, this cottage industry is somewhat urbanized, when, that is, it reaches the stage of division of labor (Figure 4-5B), the premises are expanded and a raw-materials warehouse, a warehouse for finished products, an office, living space, and the like are built separately around the factory. The area which is mere N-space in Figure 4-5A is internalized and the premises as a whole come to have "an internal order," as is shown in Figure 4-5B. When these five buildings are co-ordinated with one another and the premises are internalized, the buildings become a cluster of architecture; when any one of the five buildings functions badly, the cluster as a whole then suffers inconvenience.

When the factory is expanded farther, the living space is separated entirely from the place of work, merging into general housing and apartment houses, and the warehouses and the like are located near railway stations and wharves. When this factory employs a large commuting population, when it receives and dispatches large amounts of materials and goods, when it consumes a vast amount of energy, and when it makes frequent use of communications media such as telegraph, telephone, and TV, it is no longer a cottage industry isolated in N-space but has become closely linked with the outside society and has become part of the transportation, distribution, and communications systems of the city. If the city is small in scale, it is possible to conceive of the whole city as "an internal order" containing the factory. Generally speaking, however, it is more appropriate to think that this factory space exists in a city dominated by "an external order" based on a land-use plan, a transportation plan, and the like.

Fig. 4-5.

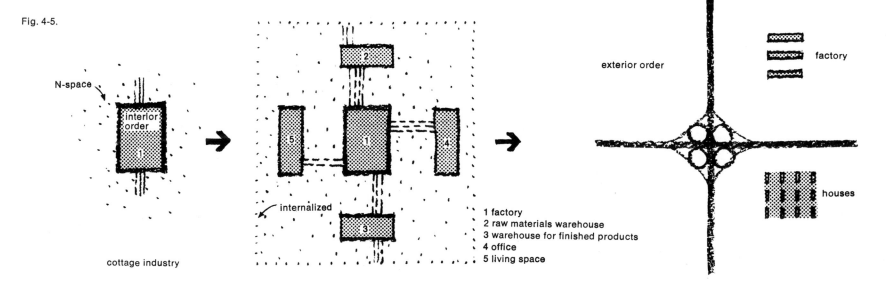

N-space

interior order

internalized

cottage industry

1 factory
2 raw materials warehouse
3 warehouse for finished products
4 office
5 living space

exterior order

factory

houses

A

B

C

When a succession of internalizations of space takes place, how far can this process proceed? It may be said that internalization continues spontaneously, on larger and larger scales, as need arises, but the co-ordinating system of internalized space develops a "hardening of the arteries" in trying to maintain an internal order at all costs. Beyond a certain point, the functions of internalized space begin to slow down and its efficiency rapidly drops; if internalization continues further unabated, the internal order simply explodes because of the internalization pressure, counterpressure develops to check internalization, or something like cell division takes places in the internal order. The idea of the birth of a second internal order as a result of "cell division" is an important one in relation to the space theory so far considered. When an internal order aggrandizes itself through internalization, it transforms itself into centrifugal and poorly co-ordinated space; when a frame to check the further growth of the internal order is brought into existence as a result of "cell division," however, space of a high quality is created centripetally. When an internal order exists, it is surrounded by N-space; when that internal

Fig. 4-6.
A. When an internal order exists, it is usually surrounded by N-space.
B. The internalization pressure develops, thus causing "cell division."
C. As a result of "cell division," a second internal order comes into existence; PN-space develops between the first and second internal orders.
D. When a great amount of "cell division" take place, it is necessary to introduce the idea of an external order.

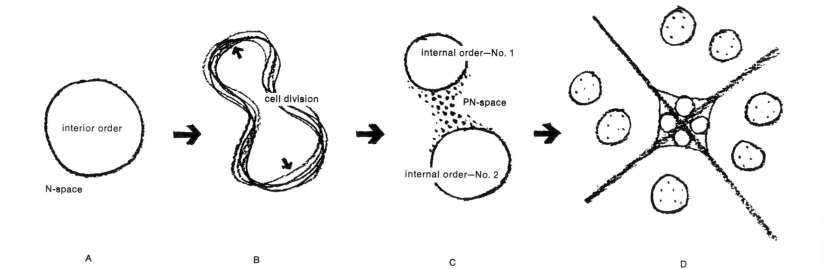

interior order

N-space

A

cell division

B

internal order—No. 1

PN-space

internal order—No. 2

C

D

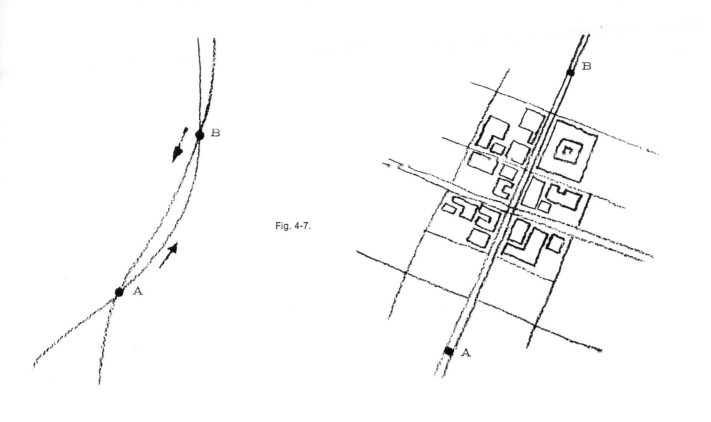

Fig. 4-7.

A road connecting A and B.

A network-type road.

order is divided into two, PN-space appears between the two internal orders. It is necessary, of course, to introduce the idea of an external order if pressure for development mounts and a great amount of "cell division" takes place.

One of the factors hampering internalization is the fragmented ownership of land in an existing city. One way to overcome this problem is to create large plots of land anew; another way is, as in the older built-up areas of American cities, to undertake urban-renewal programs. On the other hand, the method of creating an external order based on a land-use plan, a transportation plan, and the like prevents internalization from outside. Since the appearance of the automobile, for instance, roads have been specialized into two kinds: roads simply connecting, say, point A and point B, and network-type roads connecting not only point A with point B but also many buildings between the two points with each other. If the latter type is treated as part of an external order, confusion develops at the points where the roads meet clusters of buildings. It would then be much wiser to treat the road as part of an internal order, like a corridor in a building. On the other hand, the former type of road is obviously part of an external order and becomes nothing but a nuisance when placed within an internal order.

There are possibly two methods of building a city. One is to build it by internalizing space and by maintaining an internal order, which may be compared to architecture by addition. The other is to build the city by maintaining an external order of urban infrastructure, as represented by a land-use plan, a transportation plan, etc.; this method may be compared to architecture by subtraction. The city is a complex organism in which a metabolic process is always at work, and it is extremely difficult to comprehend even when it is right before our eyes. Such terms as "city planning" and "urban design" may imply somewhat different scales, contents, and methods in different disciplines. From the point of view of space theory, at any rate, it may be said that city planning is aimed at establishing a two-dimensional external order while architectural planning is aimed at creating a three-dimensional internal order. The two-dimensional external order is grasped when one views the city from many thousands of feet high in the sky; it has nothing to do with human behavior—how a man sits on a chair, with whom he dines, where he sleeps. On the other hand, the three-dimensional internal order attaches the greatest importance to human behavior, and it should be planned to meet human needs.

Jane Jacobs criticizes the "city grandiose": "Most urban redevelopment projects, give or take a few malls, promise scenes like this: pompous, formalistic patterns that look fine from the top of a tower or in architect's perspective, but will be an oppressive void to the poor pedestrian! The city is for human beings, not for a race of giant men playing a new kind of chess."[1] The situation she attacks has arisen for the following reasons: first, perhaps the designer-architect had a somewhat unclear idea of the areas to be covered by an internal order and so designed in the formalistic terms of an external order what he should have designed in the fine-grained terms of an internal order; second, perhaps he did not take into consideration the full implications of the two methods of creating order—an internal order working from the inside and an external order working from the outside—even if he chose the method of creating an external order; and third, perhaps he was extremely busy and did his design work in too great a hurry.

The argument that each part of the city becomes monotonous and inhuman unless there is mixed land use is very persuasive, but the essence of the city is the division of labor and specialization, and

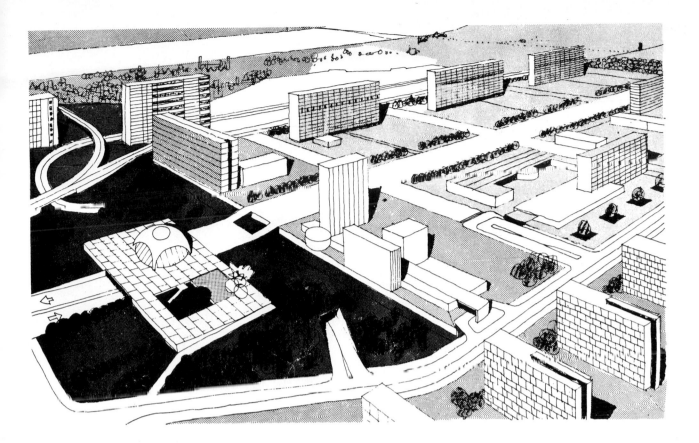

Fig. 4-8. Jane Jacobs, "City Grandiose," from *The Exploding Metropolis*, p. 159.

such trends will be reinforced in the future whether one likes them or not. It is technically impossible for an entire modern metropolis with a population of several millions to be maintained by an internal order based on mixed land use; if a metropolis were to be maintained by such an order, great confusion would arise. However, if there are many different internal orders as a result of "cell division" instead of a single internal order in the metropolis, many internal orders, each with an individuality of its own, will coexist within the external order, and efficiency and humanity will be restored.

In this connection, it is interesting to examine Louis Kahn's proposal for Philadelphia's Center City.[2] Kahn calls for the construction of huge "harbor" towers, each 440 feet in diameter, with all-day parking areas in the cores, and apartments, offices, and motels around the cores. These towers seem to suggest "an internal order" like that we have been considering. They seem to have a considerably self-sufficient order. An external order is planned around the towers, but Kahn seems to think that if the towers are built first, an external order will naturally develop in time as occasion demands. Other recent

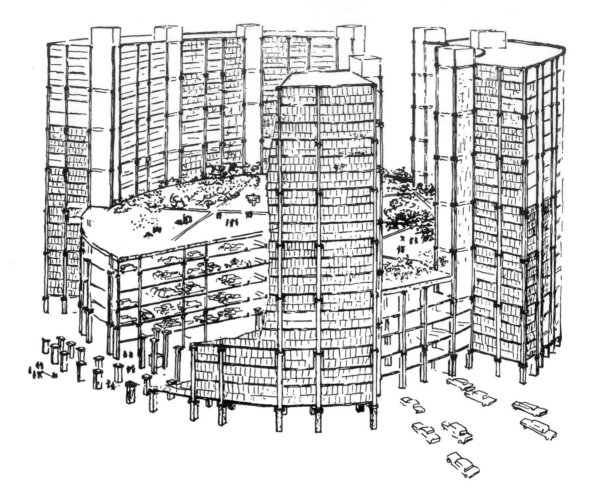

Fig. 4-9. "Louis Kahn's Proposal for Philadelphia's Center City," from *Architectural Forum,* March, 1958, p. 117.

plans for urban design have first proposed the creation of a system of an external order for the whole city and then attempted to arrange internal orders within the city; unlike such plans, Kahn's proposal calls for the creation of an internal order first and an external order next. This seems to be characteristic of an architect's way of thinking.

In Japan, people have traditionally maintained a self-sufficient, well-defined order inside their houses and set up fences around the houses to protect this internal order.[3] In the center of the Japanese house there are a Buddhist altar, which corresponds to a chapel in Western Europe, and a *tokonoma* (alcove) for displaying art objects, a place equivalent to a private museum. The Japanese custom of removing shoes on entering a house is symbolic of the internal order maintained inside the house. Since the boundaries between inside

An internal order in a traditional Japanese house.
(Photo by Yukio Futagawa)

A congested area of a Japanese city.
(Photo by Yukio Futagawa)

and outside are established at the points where man removes his shoes, people have traditionally been indifferent to space outside their houses, regarding it as N-space; since community is considered as a mere collection of small internal orders, the internalization of community space as a cluster does not take place. For example, the public space of streets often remains unpaved. On the contrary, in Western European countries people enter their houses from the street pavement without removing their shoes; the art of paving streets with beautiful patterns is, therefore, old in Europe and has been perfected, especially in Italian cities. The custom of wearing shoes symbolizes an external order. It may be said that the concept of an external order in Western European life derives from the individualism that establishes the boundaries between inside and outside at the edge of an individual's mind. In Japan, all activities corresponding to praying at a church, taking a rest in a park, dining at a restaurant, and chatting with friends on a plaza all take place inside the house.

Perhaps Japanese cities are now confused because of the lack of the concept of an external order, while Western cities are at an impasse because of the lack of the concept of an internal order. How to organize both an internal and an external order in the city, how to save it from degenerating into stagnation and inhumanity, and how to transform it into a vital and efficient organism—these are all extremely important questions. Visitors to Japan from abroad who have little experience with an internal order, including experts in city planning and architecture, seem at first confused by the complexity of Japanese cities brought about by their internal orders; however, the diversity and humanity brought about by this very complexity may well transform any sense of confusion into a feeling of great satisfaction, even ecstasy. As Nathan Glazer says, the great charm of Tokyo is its variety and vitality derived from a mixed land use.[4]

Is there any way to introduce an external order into Tokyo and at the same time to retain its variety and vitality? At present Tokyo is rapidly developing an external order without changing its mammoth size. It may be possible, however, to divide Tokyo into smaller units as internal orders—such as Tokyo No. 1, Tokyo No. 2...Tokyo No. 10 —and introduce the concept of an external order among these units. Such a method of creating an internal and an external order may also be applied in other large cities of the world such as New York and London. Although the architect's role is to translate abstract concepts into tangible form, he must study relationships between an internal and an external order that are complicated and always changing.

FOOTNOTES:

CHAPTER 1   [1]Lao Tzu:

"Though clay may be molded into a vase, the essence of the vase is in the emptiness within it. Though doors and windows may be cut to make a house, the essence of the house is in the emptiness within it. Therefore, taking advantage of what is, we recognize the essence of what is not."

[2]Paul Zucker, *Town and Square* (New York: Columbia University Press, 1959).

[3]Dora Jane Hamblin, "The World's Crookedest Horse Race," *Life,* Vol. 31, No. 4, Jul. 23, 1951.

[4]G. E. Kidder Smith, *Italy Builds* (New York: Reinhold Publishing Co., 1945), p. 47.

CHAPTER 2   [1]H. Märtens, *Der optishe Masstab in der bildenden Kunsten* (2nd edition) (Berlin: Wasmuth, 1884).

[2]H. Blumenfeld, "Scale in Civic Design," *The Town Planning Review,* Vol. XXIV 1953-1954, University Press, Liverpool.

[3]Werner Hegemann and Elbert Peets, *The American Vitruvius, an Architect's Handbook of Civic Art,* (New York: Architectural Book Publishing Co., 1922).

[4]Zucker, *op. cit.,* p. 7.

[5]Camillo Sitte, *The Art of Building Cities,* trans. by Charles T. Stewart (New York: Reinhold, 1945).

[6]Edward T. Hall, *The Silent Language* (New York: Fawcett World Library, 1963) p. 147.

[7]Sitte, *op. cit.*

[8]M. Murata and Y. Ashihara, Arch. & Assocs., "The Komazawa Olympic Park," *Japan Architect,* Nov. 1964; *Architectural Design,* Feb. 1963; *L'architecture d'aujourd'hui,* Jan. 1964; *L'architettura,* Jul. 1964; *Baumeister,* May 1964; *Shinkenchiku,* Apr. 1962, Jul. 1964, and Oct. 1964; *Kenchiku Bunka,* Jul. 1967.

[9]Y. Ashihara, Arch. & Assocs., "The Musashino Art University Library," *Japan Architect,* Jul. 1967; *Japan Interior Design,* Jul. 1967.

[10]Y. Ashihara, Arch. & Assocs., "Ibaragi Cultural Center," *Shinkenchiku,* June 1966; *Kenchiku Bunka,* June 1966; *SD,* June 1966; *Japan Interior Design,* June 1966; *Kentiku,* Jul. 1966; *Japan Architect,* Oct. 1966.

[11]Y. Ashihara, Arch. & Assocs., "Iwanami Warehouse," *Japan Architect,* Apr. 1965; *Shinkenchiku,* Feb. 1965.

CHAPTER 3

[1] Y. Ashihara, Arch. & Assocs., "Sony Building," *Shinkenchiku*, June 1966; *Kenchiku Bunka*, June 1966; *SD*, June 1966; *Japanese Interior Design*, June 1966; *Kentiku*, Jul. 1966; *Japan Architect*, Oct. 1966.

[2] Y. Ashihara, Arch. & Assocs., "Japan Pavilion at Expo 67, Montreal," *Shinkenchiku*, May 1967; *Kenchiku Bunka*, May 1967; *Design*, Jul. 1967; *SD*, Jul. 1967; *Japan Architect*, Aug. 1967; *The Architectural Review*, Aug. 1967.

[3] Y. Ashihara, Arch. & Assocs., "Kagawa Prefectural Library," *Shinkenchiku*, Apr. 1963; *Kenchiku Bunka*, Apr. 1963; *Japan Architect*, June 1963; *L'architecture d'aujourd'hui*, Apr. 1965.

[4] Y. Ashihara, Arch. & Assocs., "The Campus of the Musashino Art University," *Shinkenchiku*, Nov. 1964; *Kenchiku Bunka*, Nov. 1964; *Japan Architect*, Jan. 1965.

[5] Zucker, *op. cit.*

[6] N. Asano & Others, *Hiho-Itsukushima* (Itsukushima Shrine, the 10th volume of the *Great Treasures Series*) (Tokyo: Kodansha Publishing Co., 1967).

CHAPTER 4

[1] Jane Jacobs, "Downtown is for People" in *The Exploding Metropolis*, the Editors of *Fortune*, ed. (New York: Doubleday & Co., 1958), p. 159.

[2] "Louis Kahn and the Living City," *Architectural Forum*, March, 1958, pp. 114-119.

[3] Tetsuro Watsuji, *Fudo* (Climate) (Tokyo: Iwanami-Shoten, 1940). The English translation of this book was published by the Japanese Commission for UNESCO in 1962 as *A Climate: A Philosophical Study*.

[4] Nathan Glazer, "Nyuyoku to Tokyo o Kuraberuto" (Comparing New York and Tokyo), *Chuo-Koron*, Jan. 1962, pp. 290-297.

INDEX